Andrew
Murray

WOMEN OF FAITH SERIES

Amy Carmichael
Corrie ten Boom
Florence Nightingale
Gladys Aylward
Hannah Whitall Smith
Isobel Kuhn
Joni
Mary Slessor

MEN OF FAITH SERIES

Andrew Murray
Borden of Yale
Brother Andrew
C. S. Lewis
Charles Colson
Charles Finney
Charles Spurgeon
D. L. Moody
Eric Liddell
George Muller
Hudson Taylor
Jim Elliot
Jonathan Goforth
John Hyde
John Newton
John Paton
John Wesley
Martin Luther
Samuel Morris
Terry Waite
William Carey
William Booth

John and Betty Stam

Andrew Murray

Dr. William Lindner, Jr.

BETHANY HOUSE PUBLISHERS
MINNEAPOLIS, MINNESOTA 55438

Published by Bethany House Publishers
A Ministry of Bethany Fellowship, Inc.
11300 Hampshire Avenue South
Minneapolis, Minnesota 55438

Printed in the United States of America

Library of Congress Cataloging-in-Publication Data

Lindner, William.
    Andrew Murray / William Lindner, Jr.
        p.   cm. — (Men of faith)

    1. Murray, Andrew, 1828–1917. 2. Nederduitse
Gereformeerde Kerk—Clergy—Biography.
3. Reformed Church—South Africa—Clergy—
Biography. 4. Evangelists—South Africa—Biography.
5. Devotional literature, English—History and
criticism. I. Title. II. Series.
BX9622.Z8M875   1996
284'.2'092—dc20
[B]   95–25904
ISBN 1–55661–670–8   CIP

To everyone who had hoped to one day
meet the man behind the books.

DR. WILLIAM LINDNER, JR. holds a D.Min. on renewal, with an emphasis on the ministry of Andrew Murray. He is a pastor in the Evangelical Presbyterian Church and ministers with the Presbyterian and Reformed Renewal Ministries. He lives in Michigan with his wife and three children.

Contents

1

To Scotland: Uncle John, University, and the First Winds of Revival

The Murray Brothers were hardly prone to weeping. Still, it must have been difficult for John and Andrew, ages twelve and ten, not to be touched by a note of sadness as they stood on the ship pulling away from the harbor in Port Elizabeth. Surely this trip halfway around the world to Scotland, and the education that would come with it, was a rare privilege. The voyage was to be long and hazardous, the duration of their studies unknown. It would be understandably hard for a ten-year-old boy to think of adventure when the happy life he had known was receding in the distance.

Andrew Murray, Sr., Andrew's father, came to South Africa as a missionary in July 1822. He was the second son of a Scottish family marked by deep "Old Light" Presbyterian convictions. Upon completion of his university studies in preparation for ministry, Andrew, Sr., had stayed close to home in deference to his beloved mother's wishes.

Meanwhile, the British had taken control of the Cape of Good Hope and the Colony of South Africa. In doing so, they had inherited oversight of the Dutch Reformed Church in South Africa, which was in great need of ministers. Owing to the many similarities between the Dutch Reformed and Scottish Presbyterian faiths, the government turned to Scotland to recruit willing ministers for the task. For Mr. Murray it was a call that could not be refused. At the urging of Dr. George Thom, he pulled up stakes, boarded a ship, and headed for South Africa, never again to see Scotland.

Assigned to the church in Graaf-Reinet, Mr. Murray settled in quickly to his ministry. Within the first year, he had mastered the Dutch language, even able to preach fluently in it. The very next year, while attending the General Synod meeting of the Dutch Reformed Church meeting in Cape Town, Mr. Murray would meet Maria Stegmann. They married the year after that, when she was still only sixteen years old. With that the Murray roots were firmly planted in the new country. Andrew, Sr., would serve this same Graaf-Reinet church for the next forty-five years until he retired at the age of seventy. So deep was his affiliation with his new country that his children could never recall his ever expressing a desire to return to the land of his birth.

The Murray home was a happy one. Eleven children grew up in the spacious parsonage, Andrew being the second. Most would either become or marry ministers. Mr. Murray, though no tyrant, was the head of the household in the old-fashioned way. His counsel was sought and followed in all matters.

Mr. Murray had a genuine tenderness for each child's spiritual condition. Andrew's sister would recall in a letter:

> Our father's conversations with his children were very instructive. His sons remember rides with him upon which he told them many interesting things connected with natural history or geography. The occasions on which he spoke to his children about their souls were few but well chosen, and his words never failed to make an impression. It was generally on a Sabbath evening after family worship when the child came for a good-night kiss. "Well, dearie, have you given your heart to Christ yet?" or, "Will you not, before you go to bed tonight, give yourself to Jesus?" Or on a birthday he would say, "This is your birthday: are you born again?" One thing that impressed us particularly was that he expected that the elder children should interest themselves in the soul's welfare of the younger ones. To a married daughter, visiting her old home, he said, "Have you spoken to the little girls about their souls yet? I wish you would do so."
>
> Many words of Scripture became engraven on the hearts of the children through hearing their father repeat them with great feeling and emphasis. Indeed, he has left them to us as a most precious legacy. The word of Christ did indeed dwell in him richly, and he taught and admonished us in psalms and hymns and spiritual songs, singing with grace in his heart unto the Lord.

Mrs. Murray was a bright and contented person. Only twenty when Andrew was born, she maintained a close relationship with all of her children. She was always busy and fulfilled in her love of God, her husband, and her children.

How can a child attempt to describe a mother, and especially such a mother? To us she never seemed at all like anyone else; she was just *Mama*. She taught us to read before we were old enough to be sent to school, and the hymns and verses that we learned at her knee have remained in the memory for a lifetime. When our father was from home, Mama took upon herself the task of hearing the boys repeat their lessons before going to school. One of her sons still remembers how, when he grumbled at his difficult Latin lesson, Mama learned the lesson with him, and made him take the book while she repeated it, and so encouraged him.

On Sunday she taught us the *Kort Begrip* (Shorter Catechism). It is sweet to recall those Sundays. Such Sabbath-keeping has gone out of fashion. Children now would perhaps think it a weariness, yet we cannot remember that we as children ever did. The day was strictly observed.

There was a deep sense of communion with God that pervaded the household. Mrs. Murray was not to be disturbed during her private devotions, and Mr. Murray devoted every Friday night to prayer for revival. He would adjourn to his study to pray and to read of former revivals in Scotland and other countries. Andrew vividly recalled from his youngest days standing outside the door and hearing his father's deep travail for that same blessing in his own church and time.

Graaf-Reinet was one of the most important towns in the Cape province, situated on a well-watered plain in the midst of the dry inland plateau known as the Karoo, 500 miles northeast of Cape Town. It was a regular stopping place for travelers making their way into the interior. Many missionaries, Dr. Livingstone and Dr. Moffatt in particular, were house guests while the children were growing up.

It had been a difficult decision for Reverend and Mrs. Murray to send their two eldest sons away for their education. The schools in South Africa at this time were very limited in their curriculum, however, and the boys each showed great academic promise. In addition, there was their Uncle John, Mr. Murray's brother in Aberdeen, Scotland, who could open his home to them for as long as it might take.

The boys arrived in the autumn of 1838 after a four-month voyage that could only be described as miserable. Their studies began the very next day. And study they did. Over the next seven years John and Andrew worked hard. Their natural ability and the solid foundation of their home education helped them to achieve consistent honors in the Scottish college. They graduated together in 1845, Andrew being only seventeen years old!

The boys must have found their new home agreeable, though somewhat different from that of their parents back in South Africa. Their mother was cheerful and contented, but their aunt was of a noticeably more depressed temperament. But, like their father, their uncle was a fortress of strength. Years later, Andrew would remember his uncle's kindness and stability in sometimes trying circumstances as inspiration with his own ministry to those pressed by doubt and temptation.

The boys enjoyed a close and amicable relationship with their four cousins. The brief reminisces of cousin Isabella give a fascinating glimpse into their lives and manner:

> [Andrew] was a bright, lovable boy, extremely obliging, and devoted to his brother John, to whom he owed much. John was studious and thoughtful beyond his years, and seemed weighted with a sense of responsibility, both on his own account and Andrew's. . . . One remarkable thing I can tell you, which applies to both boys—with neither of them had their uncle and aunt even once to find fault during their eight years' stay in our house, and this was due, we believed, to incessant prayer for them in the Graaf-Reinet home. We, the younger members of the family, looked on them as brothers, and were brokenhearted when they left us.

Great things were happening outside the Murray household at this time as well. Scotland was being touched by a wave of revival, similar to those in the United States under the ministry of Charles Finney. Because their uncle John was a well-known minister of evangelical inclination, both boys had opportunity to see the events and participants close at hand.

The Murrays became associated with the so-called Free Church, an evangelical movement that separated from the State Church in a dispute referred to as "the Disruption." In Aberdeen, where the Murrays lived, the Free Church adherents had been worshiping outdoors in a tent with some 2,000 people regularly in attendance. One Sunday, word was received that the saintly college professor Dr. Thomas Chalmers was to preach. Two hours before the service the tent was crowded, with many more people gathered around. What could they do but move the entire event to an open-air setting? There Dr. Chalmers preached to some 10,000 people "by whom he was completely heard." Both boys were no doubt part of this memorable event.

Reverend William C. Burns was another renowned preacher of the day. Known for prayer and fasting, Burns seemed to all who met him to carry a sense of God's presence that overwhelmed what he lacked in preaching style. "If his words were sometimes few, naked, unadorned, they were full of weight and power, and went home as arrows directed by a sure aim to the heart and consciences of his hearers."

Burns was a regular houseguest of the Murrays and soon took a personal interest in the two young boys. Andrew even served by carrying Burns's coat and Bible as they walked together to meetings. The open and direct style of this great man of God can be seen in this letter to John:

> Do not, I beseech you, give way to the secret thought that you are excusable in remaining in your present unrenewed state, or that there is

the smallest possible hope of your being saved unless you are really born of the Holy Spirit, and reconciled to the Holy Jehovah by the atoning blood of His only-begotten Son. Search your heart, my dear fellow-sinner, and I am sure that you will find something which you are refusing to let go at the command of God. . . .

P.S. Show this to Andrew, whom it may also suit.

John and Andrew were fourteen and twelve when they received this letter in response to their own separate letters of inquiry. No doubt such a piercing word from so respected a mentor would have had lasting impact on each boy's development.

While young students in Scotland, both John and Andrew began to consider their life's vocation. It was their father, Andrew, Sr., back in South Africa, who seems to have had the deepest influence on their decisions. He was half a world away, with letters often three months in time between writing and delivery. The boys had a deep respect for their father and considered carefully every word of advice they received. In addition, their parents' prayer life seemed to overcome the distance in miles, providing a gentle, ever-present affirmation that was vividly real.

Andrew, Sr., encouraged both boys to consider pursuits that would capitalize on their unique education. Why travel to Scotland for these many years, only to pursue a trade that they could have learned just as well in South Africa? Avoid the legal profession due to the scandalous lack of principles and morals that marked the South African bar, he said. "Should you feel inclined to turn your attention to theology or medicine or mercantile pursuits, I have no doubt there will always be openings at the Cape, as well as at other places. If I were in your circumstances, I should cast an eye toward the Indian Missions: *there* is something worthy the ambitions of great minds."

In the end, both boys chose to pursue further study in theology with the ministry in mind. Their family was delighted. Once again, it was their father's wise advice that helped them through the next series of decisions. "Study in Holland," he would say, "as much for the language as for the theology." And so it was. June of 1845 found the Murray boys, now a good bit older and more mature, boarding a ship in pursuit of education once again. This time from Scotland to Holland!

2

Called and Converted: Studies in Holland

And watch out for their abominable customs of drinking gin and water, and smoking tobacco and cigars. Entertain your friends with tea and coffee. Holland is famous for both. Don't be afraid to be different." These words of advice from Andrew Murray, Sr., to his sons must have tempered their excitement with a dose of reality!

It was June of 1845. At seventeen, Andrew and his brother John were sailing from Scotland for Holland. There they would begin theological studies at the University of Utrecht.

The senior Murray's letters of fatherly advice continued: "When I went to Holland, they overcharged me because I didn't speak Dutch." His sons arrived forewarned, but in much the same condition. Andrew and John could speak English well, but their Dutch was weak. Initially, their conversation with other students was conducted in the academic language of the day, Latin.

The two boys from the faraway Dutch colony of South Africa must have been quite the sight upon their arrival in Holland. One of their soon-to-be friends would later remember: "There were two youths in somewhat strange garb walking along the streets with cheerful countenances and unassuming demeanor. . . . Whether their Latin was classically pure, or even intelligible or endurable, is open to question. But it was sufficient and we understood one another."

Holland of the mid-nineteenth century was a treacherous place for two young men. Their father was all too aware of this as well.

> You may soon hear sentiments broached among the students, and even by professors, on theological subjects which may startle you, but be cautious in receiving them, by whatever names or number of names they may be supported. Try to act like the noble Bereans (Acts 17:11). By studying your Bibles and your own hearts I doubt not, under the guidance of the blessed Spirit, you will be led into all truth.

Months later, Andrew, Sr., would receive a letter from his son that would confirm his worst fears about Dutch student life, even while confirming his highest hopes for the discernment of his namesake. Andrew wrote home:

> Above all, I forgot to mention the scandalous morals of the theological students. I solemnly assure you the name of God is profaned in the theological classroom, even by the orthodox and respectable students; nor do they lose character by being intoxicated now and then on some festive occasion, provided only it does not take place immediately before the *proponents-*

examen (examination for license). And in this I take no notice of grosser offenses of which a few are guilty, who, though destitute of character and notorious, still become ministers when they are ready.

Church life in Holland had grown cold and formal, deeply impacted by the growing rationalism of the time. This impacted the training that both boys would receive. Andrew wrote home concerning one professor:

His attitude toward revelation may be gauged by his assertion that "there is no room for miracle, either in the series of natural phenomena or in the fabric of human existence: for every fact, whether in the realm of nature or in the world of humanity, some physical or human cause exists (though, perhaps, as yet unknown) which can account for it."

As always though, God had His witness. Even in the spiritually arid climate of Holland, there were some stirrings of revival. A movement known as *Reveil* had spilled over into Dutch church life from Switzerland, decades before the arrival of John and Andrew. It had been primarily a result of the informal evangelistic work and Bible readings among Swiss theological students by two Scottish brothers, James and Robert Haldane. The movement came to Holland by way of several well-known professors and Jewish converts whose lives had been deeply touched by God. While clearly a minority view, and influential more in literary circles than among church officials, the *Reveil* had spawned a small fellowship of theological students on the cam-

pus of Utrecht in 1843, two years before Andrew
and John arrived. These students covenanted together "to promote the study of the subjects required for the ministerial calling in the spirit of the
Revival."

Earnest in their Christian faith, they chose the
name *Zechar Debar* from the Hebrew, meaning "Remember the Word." Their fellow students had a
number of different names for them though!
Shunned by classmates, this small band of evangelical students was renamed "The Chocolate Club"
for their decision to not serve wine or liquor at their
meetings. Their convictions on many things did not
escape comment from the more liberal faculty. Andrew's brother John remembered the advice of a
certain Professor Royaards "not to allow the *Zechar
Debar* society to gain too great an influence over
him, lest he should expose himself to the danger of
fanaticism."

The similarities between the *Zechar Debar* and
the Holy Clubs that John and Charles Wesley had
been involved with more than a hundred years earlier, while students at Oxford, are many. A church
historian named Bolleine would write of *Zechar Debar*:

> "This was the problem which they discussed
> night after night—by what rules ought a Chris-
> tian to regulate his life? They tried to map out
> for each week a sort of railway timetable, hav-
> ing a fixed and definite duty for every moment
> of the day; and the revision and perfection of
> their timetables occupied much of their eve-
> nings. As the rumor of what they were doing
> spread through the colleges, it appealed to the

loose-living men around them as a tremendous
joke. Dozens of nicknames were coined, but one
young gentleman of Christ Church unearthed
for them an old name which was destined to become historic. "Here is a new sect of Method-
ists," he sneered.

The *Zechar Debar* stands out as an important
and formative moment in the life of Andrew Murray and his brother John. Indeed, a relatively large
number of the South African students found their
way to the group over the years. Here they found
fellowship and evangelical encouragement while
forging a faith that would influence the Dutch Reformed Church of South Africa through their leadership for many decades to come.

No doubt *Zechar Debar* helped develop Andrew's lifelong commitment to the ministry with
students. Here a seed grew, matured, and later in
his life produced more seed that would in turn be
planted to become the foundation of student groups
like today's InterVarsity Christian Fellowship.

Zechar Debar was far more than a withdrawn
and isolated band of conservative students. Much of
their free time was given to serving others in the
name of Christ. On Sunday afternoons, they often
gathered the children of the poorest families in the
city for Bible lessons and worship in what must
have been much like the Sunday schools that would
blossom years later. Time that other students gave
to recreation was invested in visitation and exhortation. There was also a zealous missionary spirit
among the members of *Zechar Debar*. John and
Andrew were instrumental in establishing another

student group—*Eletheto*—a study group focused on missionary matters.

For all their time of study and activity, the years in Utrecht were also of important personal development for Andrew. In the words of his colleague and biographer, it was "at Utrecht [that] he underwent the great change which he called his conversion, and which made him more definitely the Lord's. He used to say that he could point to the very house, the very room, and, of course, the very date when this change ensued. His conversion was no sudden upheaval, but it was a distinct and complete surrender to Christ and to His claims—a clear-cut experience from which he dated a new era, and which lay at the foundation of all the preaching of later years."

As sons of a devout missionary-pastor, both John and Andrew Murray grew up in a solid Christian home. They both understood and were personally committed to an orthodox biblical theology. They gave themselves to solid Christian activities and fellowship. Now in Holland, they were even excelling in studies for the ministry. Certainly, by all outward appearances, they were both young men of exemplary Christian character. All of their upbringing, study, and conviction brought them to another important conviction as well. Authentic conversion, that feeling of a "heart strangely warmed," was a unique work of God to be earnestly sought after, though it could only be sovereignly given and humanly received.

No outward human activity, no matter how good or how godly, was to be confused with the deep inner work of the new birth. Indeed, Andrew's own father had this in mind when he responded to the news that Andrew was going to Utrecht to prepare for the ministry:

I have now to congratulate you on your choice of a profession, and rejoice that the Lord has been pleased to incline your heart the way He has done. I trust, however, my dear boy, that you have given your heart to Jesus Christ, to be His now and His forever, to follow Him through good and through bad report.

From his parents, his uncle John, and the evangelists that both he and John had met in Scotland, Andrew had come to see the importance and necessity of a definite experience of grace upon complete surrender to Christ.

In a letter to his parents dated November 14, 1845, Andrew first broke the joyous news.

My Dear Parents,

It was with very great pleasure that I today received your letter of August 15, containing the announcement of the birth of another brother. And equal, I am sure, will be your delight when I tell you that I can communicate to you far gladder tidings, over which angels have rejoiced, that your son has been born again. . . .

When I look back to see how I have been brought to where I now am, I must acknowledge that I see nothing. "He hath brought the blind by a way that he knew not, and led him in a path that he hath not known." For the last two or three years there has been a process going on. . . . And though I cannot yet say that I have had anything of that deep special sight into the guiltiness of sin which many people appear to have, yet I trust, and at present I feel as if I could say, I am confident that as a sinner I have been led to cast myself on Christ.

Months later, on the eve of his eighteenth birthday, Andrew would again write his parents concerning his own moment of turning.

Tomorrow will close a year that is certainly the most eventful in my life, a year in which I have been made to experience most abundantly that God is good to the soul that seeketh Him. And oh! What goodness it is when He himself implants in us the desire to seek Him while we are yet enemies. I rather think that when I last wrote I gave an account of what I believed was my conversion, and, God be thanked, I still believe that it was His work. Since the letter I cannot say that I have always had as much enjoyment as before it, but still there has been much joy in the Lord, though, alas, there has also been much sin. . . . But through grace I have always been enabled to trust in Him who has begun the good work in me, and to believe that He will also perform what He has, out of His free love before I was born, begun. Oh! That I might receive grace to walk more holy before Him.

3

First Steps Toward Ministry

With their studies in Holland nearing an end, the Murray brothers faced a time of momentous decisions. Andrew in particular was faced with challenging circumstances, due to his young age. Only twenty years old, there seemed little chance of his being ordained for at least two more years. What was he to do?

His inclination was to move to Germany for further theological studies. He had enough of the rationalistic lectures of Utrecht and hoped to find a different spiritual climate in Germany. Andrew wrote specifically of his interest in the school at Halle. The university there was still warmed by the ministry of August Franke and the German pietists that had centered there some 150 years earlier. "There are a great many excellent (both in head and heart) professors, at the head of whom stands Tholuck, a pious man, professor of exegesis," wrote Andrew. In addition to all, the cost of living was much more affordable.

Germany had already been the place of another

interesting encounter. Once, during a vacation from their classes, the brothers had taken a long walking tour along the Rhine River with friends. During the tour, they had opportunity to meet Pastor Blumhardt. This remarkable man had been used of God to bring a move of revival to the Renish provinces in Germany. It was a revival marked by the great power of God with such expressions as the exorcism of demons and healing of the sick through prayer. Andrew saw firsthand the ongoing work of God's power in his own time. One can see God at work through this encounter, putting another piece of their own education in revival into place.

For all of Andrew's interest in Germany, his father was not convinced, and in the end, his counsel prevailed. "There are spheres of usefulness here from the time one arrives, and one is gaining experience before he has all the responsibility of a congregation," wrote Andrew's father. He even wrote to his son about missionary-type opportunities along South Africa's vast frontier.

In the end, much of the concern turned out to be for naught. On May 9, 1848, Andrew's twentieth birthday, the Hague Committee of the Dutch Reformed Church broke with their long-standing precedent and ordained the two Murray brothers together! Andrew was the youngest candidate for ministry ever ordained.

Departing Utrecht for South Africa was not without its sorrow and farewells to the collection of students that made up *Zechar Debar*.

"Our time to depart has come," said John solemnly.

It was Sunday afternoon, July 3, 1848. Fifteen

of the *Zechar Debar* students had gathered for a time of farewell to the Murrays in the rooms of one of the members. The next day, one of the students wrote his fiancee of the experience, saying, "It was our united and fervent desire to show forth the Lord's death at the Sacramental Table, and to declare our expectation of His return."

John Murray opened their time together by leading them in the singing of a favorite hymn: "Evermore Will I Sing of God's Mercies." Next they prayed, and then read together the scriptural institution of the Lord's Supper. It was a touching and holy moment, one that would be remembered by all present for years to come. Amidst the spontaneous prayer and confession of faith, John once again led them in song: "Jesus, in Thine Atoning Death Our Heart Confides and Rests."

Then came time to receive the elements, "and thus held communion with the body and blood of Christ, who died for our sins and was raised for our justification. We ate and drank and were indeed strengthened and quickened."

Again, John led the group. He read from Psalm 103 and Colossians 3, "Since, then, you have been raised with Christ, set your hearts on things above, where Christ is seated at the right hand of God." After a prayer of thanksgiving and words of encouragement to one another, the group sang Psalm 133 together. "How good and pleasant it is when brothers live together in unity!" With a benediction, they departed.

Later that evening, at seven o'clock, they gathered once again at the family home of one of their members, Mr. N. H. deGraf. Mr. deGraf opened the meeting with prayer and singing, and then read portions of Romans 16: "Now to him who is able to establish you by my gospel and the proclamation of Jesus Christ. . . . To the only wise God be glory forever through Jesus Christ!" Until dinner at nine, the young men spent time in fellowship and final farewells.

Upon completion of the meal at ten, those present gathered together in worship and the reading of the Word. They sang together portions of Psalm 116: "I love the LORD, for he heard my voice; he heard my cry for mercy," followed by the reading of Ephesians 1 and 2 and some reflections by their host.

> We then knelt down, and I had the privilege of leading in prayer, in which I expressed the gratitude that filled the hearts of us all for the inexpressibly precious blessings we had enjoyed, especially during the past three years; and also for the blessings of this last day, when we were able to commend our beloved friends to the love of our God, with whom is no variableness or shadow of turning. We then united in singing Psalm 134 ("Lift up your hands in the sanctuary and praise the LORD!") standing close round John and Andrew. We wept and embraced the brothers so dearly beloved. John then extended his hands over our head: "The grace of our Lord Jesus Christ, the love of God and the communion of the Holy Spirit be with you all. Amen."

The brothers' trip home took them by way of Scotland and the home of their uncle John. They were received with open hearts, celebrating their successful education and ordination. Both were given the honor of preaching in their uncle's pulpit, and all who heard them were deeply moved to see the two who had come to them as young boys from the farthest of colonies, now proclaiming God's Word with great authority and conviction. Their uncle John wrote of the moment that "the family and congregation were divided in opinion as to which of the 'twa laddies' was the grander preacher." Clearly, God had great things in store for them both!

If the voyage from Scotland to South Africa was uneventful, their landing certainly was not. The arrival of two new ministers was an occasion of great importance. Family, church officials, and the press all hailed their arrival home in the grandest of terms. Though their parents were unable to meet their ship, the boys were received by their maternal grandparents and uncle. As was the custom, they were invited to preach at the *Groote Kerk*, the oldest church building in the colony.

Their journey was not done, however, until they arrived at the family home in Graaf-Reinet. Half of Andrew's life had been lived away from this place. It was his father's house, though, and that was enough to make it Andrew's home. Once home, his happy, playful disposition soon overcame his weighty minister's propriety. Brothers and sisters, several of whom he had never seen, hardly knew what to make of the new presence. "Is Brother Andrew a minister? That could never be: he's just like one of us!" they exclaimed.

There would be no doubt about the depth and seriousness of the newly returned brothers' faith.

On the first Sunday back, each son preached and then, together, the three ministers served Communion. Father and sons served the tables one after the other in rotation.

When it was Andrew's turn to dispense the elements and deliver the customary brief address, he rose, closed his eyes, and for some moments seemed lost in meditation and prayer. An almost painful silence filled the building, and a hush of deep solemnity fell upon the great assemblage. When at length the youth— for he was little more than a youth—opened his mouth, the words which he uttered were so evidently sincere, so intense and so uplifting, that those who heard him, and had last seen him as a boy of ten, could scarce restrain their tears. It was manifest to all that in these two young men God had bestowed upon His Church in South Africa a gift of inestimable value.

4

Into the Wilderness

Y ou are the elder," said Sir Harry Smith, the British governor of South Africa to John Murray. "And therefore I will give you the charge of Burgersdorp."

The British had taken over the colony of South Africa from the Dutch in 1815, seven years before Andrew's father moved there from Scotland. Up until that time, the Dutch Reformed Church in the colony had been closely intertwined with the ruling government, as was typical of European state-churches. The Church was part of the civil establishment and its ministers were simply a particular class of civil employee. With the coming of British rule, the Dutch Reformed Church in South Africa increasingly became the main pillar of Dutch colonial culture: their language, heritage, and national aspirations. The British colonial government, however, stepped into the place of the Dutch government with regard to oversight in the church. All ministerial appointments were made, not by the call of the individual congregation, but by the personal appointment of the governor. When the Murray brothers arrived back in South Africa, they

were each interviewed by then Governor Sir Harry
Smith in consideration for appointments within the
Dutch Reformed Church in South Africa.

John was given a well-settled and respected
charge, that of Burgersdorp along the eastern frontier, within the bounds of the Cape Colony. It was a
highly considered and much-sought-after appointment.

"And as you are the younger," said the governor
turning to Andrew, "I am afraid I will have to send
you to Bloemfontein." Bloemfontein! We can only
guess what Andrew's first thought must have been.
If his brother John's appointment was an esteemed
one, Andrew's was hardly known.

The early history of the colony of South Africa
was a series of confrontations between British and
Dutch settlers across expanding portions of the
southern African continent. The first of these confrontations resulted in a mass migration occurring
roughly between 1836 and 1841 and is referred to
as the Great Trek. Angered by the oppressive colonial rule of the British and resentful of what they
considered as low compensation for the forced
emancipation of slaves in 1834, the sturdy Dutch
settlers, known as Boers, packed up and moved into
the northern interior. While frequently displacing
and exchanging hostilities with various African
tribal groups, the Boers carved out homelands in
what are now called the Orange Free State, the
Transvaal and northern Natal, held together by a
republican form of government.

Not to be left behind, the British governor, the
same Sir Harry Smith who appointed the Murray
brothers, proclaimed the Queen's authority over a

large portion of these Boer lands in 1848, and annexed them to the Cape Colony as the Orange River Sovereignty. A brief but fierce military engagement between the Boers and the British took place in late August 1848, breaking the back of Boer resistance. Any survivors unable to tolerate British rule simply moved farther on, while the rest settled back into their farms and family life as best they could. The town of Bloemfontein was established as the seat of government in the annexed territory and reinforced with Royal soldiers.

Barely a year later, in 1849, Andrew Murray became the Dutch Reformed pastor in Bloemfontein. His parish, along with its political challenges, covered some 50,000 square miles of land, thinly colonized (from 12,000 to 20,000 Boers) by fiercely independent and suspicious farmers.

Imagine, if you can, spreading a small town of people over a territory just smaller than the entire state of North Carolina. Make the people devout in a traditional manner and the territory wild and unsettled, far beyond the wildest of the unsettled American West. Spread large groups of displaced tribal people across all of this territory. Now establish a single pastor over it all, a young man of barely twenty-one years who has just graduated from seminary and returned to the country after being gone nearly half of his life. This is in essence what the governor did when he said to Andrew, "I will have to send you to Bloemfontein!"

It was the customary responsibility of the church receiving a new minister to provide transport for him and his belongings to the new place of ministry. The day came in April 1849, when a huge wagon drawn by a team of large and powerful horses arrived at the Sr. Murray's home in Graaf-Reinet to pick up the new minister of Bloemfontein.

One can hardly imagine a more striking contrast than that of the coarse Dutch pioneers and the beardless young minister they had come to pick up. Yet, with an entourage of fifty mounted men from Graaf-Reinet to see them off, Andrew, his father, and the farmers loaded up Andrew's meager belongings and turned around for the three-hundred-mile journey to Bloemfontein.

Though Bloemfontein is now a well-established city and judicial seat of the Republic of South Africa, in Andrew's first days there it was at the most meager of beginnings. An English missionary passing through the town just a year after Andrew's installation leaves us this description:

> Bloemfontein, the seat of the government in this Sovereignty, has nothing to recommend it in its natural features. The scenery is extremely uninteresting. There is no wood and little water. The plan of a town is laid out. The foundation of a church is laid. A courthouse and a prison exist. There are about forty or fifty tolerable houses built. . . . There is also a government schoolhouse, but at the time of my visit without scholars or masters.

The surrounding countryside was as wild as the village was rough. Game of every sort abounded: gnus, springboks, ostriches, wild pigs, and rabbits provided food for the leopards, wolves, and wild dogs that roamed freely. Even mail routes through the area were scheduled to avoid undue exposure to lions!

Relations between the Boer farmers and their African neighbors were tense as well. Cattle poaching and boundary disputes between Boer and African as well as between African and African kept life in a constant state of upset.

The Sunday of May 6 was set as the date for Andrew's induction to the congregation at Bloemfontein. Owing to the great distance, his father was the only other Dutch Reformed minister present. Andrew, Sr., preached the charge to his son in the presence of the congregation from 2 Corinthians 6:1: "As God's fellow workers we urge you not to receive God's grace in vain." That afternoon, Andrew, Jr., preached from the text 1 Corinthians 1:23: "But we preach Christ crucified . . . Christ the power of God and the wisdom of God." At the conclusion of this service, Andrew's father directed words of encouragement and exhortation to the British inhabitants of Bloemfontein in English.

It was a time of solemn but great rejoicing for the citizens of Bloemfontein, for Andrew's installation represented both the arrival of a new minister and the recognition by the British Governor of the religious needs of the Boer people. A local parishioner, writing in a church publication, caught the moment in these words:

> It is very gratifying to learn from so many sources that the Reverend Mr. Andrew Murray is so worthy a gentleman, and moreover so well-fitted for the sphere of work assigned him.

He can rest assured that he will be welcomed in our midst in heartiest fashion. All the Boers whom I have recently met are rejoicing at the prospect of soon possessing a permanent minister.

On the Tuesday after his induction in Bloemfontein, Andrew and his father would continue on for nearly two weeks of travel and ministry on horseback. They were to ride on to Burgersdorp for John Murray's induction on the next Sunday. The trip—with some days as long as fourteen hours riding—was Andrew's first look at his extensive parish. Along the way, they would stop at farmhouses, a French Mission station, and small settlements for introductions and ministry. At every place the senior Murray would present his son with a mixture of hope, conviction, and fatherly fear. Finally, the time came for Andrew, Sr., to return to his own ministry in Graaf-Reinet. Taking the hands of two elders, the father placed his young son's own hands in them, saying, "Deal gently with the young man." Andrew Murray was now the pastor at Bloemfontein.

Andrew proved to be an energetic and active pastor. As a frontier town, Bloemfontein was full of opportunities. First, he had to make housing arrangements until a parsonage could be secured. Then work began on the church building, a project which took several years to complete. In the meantime, services were held in the school building.

As one might expect, Andrew was just as diligent with the spiritual welfare of all the people. Of course there were the Sunday services in Dutch. Andrew quickly initiated services in English as well. These were particularly challenging, as many of the British were military personnel far removed from their homes, given to drunkenness and loose morals. Just as quickly, he began services for English-speaking Africans.

Next, there was the Sunday school to be established. Early on he realized that they had many students, but few teachers! Andrew quickly began to enlist teachers, both in Dutch and English, from his congregation to teach both adults and children. Always with a heart for those whom others would overlook, Andrew even found means for instruction of the illiterate and for Bible classes among the families of native Bushmen and Hottentots.

Andrew was soon a recognized and leading citizen of the community. He was instrumental in the founding of a branch of the Temperance Society. He helped recruit teachers to schools in the area and urged the building of a library in the town.

For all of this activity, Andrew was still first and foremost a pastor. In a letter to his brother, shortly after their inductions, he stated this quite clearly and passionately:

> Now that I am getting a little settled down, I trust that our gracious God is bringing me somewhat to feel the necessity of an intimate experimental soul-knowledge of the precious truth to be proclaimed, and, above all, of that one glorious central truth—the amazing wonder of the love of a crucified Jesus. Let us, my dear brother, seek to drink much at the fountainhead, to make the love of Christ the ground

of a continual trust and hope and rejoicing.
Then shall we know what to preach to perish-
ing sinners. Then shall we also know how to
preach, with the earnestness of a burning love
that is straining every nerve to save souls.

This heart aflame for Christ showed through
Andrew's ministry with great, holy power. Though
Bloemfontein was the site of weekly Sunday services, the vast majority of Boer immigrants in the
area lived too far away to participate on any sort of
regular basis. They would instead plan to be present for the quarterly communion services held at
the church. Some would travel two weeks by oxcart
to worship, buy supplies, and renew acquaintances.
On these weekends it was not uncommon for Andrew to conduct nine services. Along with the
preaching and administration of the Sacrament, he
would baptize the newborns, sometimes as many as
fifty or a hundred in a weekend. There were mar-
riages to be conducted and youth to instruct, examine, and confirm for church membership. The
stream of people must have seemed endless.

Andrew's ministry during these events was far
more than form or tradition. He was personally involved in the instruction and examination of each
person. Time was given to private exhortation
when there was need. Motives were prayerfully dis-
cerned. When necessary, requests for baptism or
confirmation would be rejected, some "on account of
their defective knowledge; others who were lacking
in earnestness and had not really sought to believe
in Christ."

As for the service itself, one can only imagine

the awesome power of God's presence that must have been felt by everyone involved. The crowds were larger than any existing hall could hold, so services were held outdoors under the majestic African sky. As many as six large tables would be set up, around which the participants sat. After a time of hymn-singing, prayer, and preaching, people would come forward and Andrew, assisted by the elders, would instruct, pray, and distribute the bread and wine to each table.

The intense personal ministry during the Communion weekends was the fruit of a tireless commitment to pastoral visitations by Andrew. His weeks were spent traversing the many miles of his parish, sharing life and Christ with otherwise forgotten people.

They could hardly help but be drawn to the God who had sent them this fearless and unassuming pastor. No longer forgotten, the Boers must have met in Andrew something of an incarnation of God's own love and holiness.

Imagine the holy terror of one Boer family upon Andrew's visit. Surrounded by territory known to be inhabited by vicious, wild dogs, they were surprised to receive a visit from their young minister, slightly behind schedule and on foot. They soon discovered that while resting, Andrew's horse had caught scent of a pack of dogs and bolted off, leaving Andrew without a mount.

"How did you make it here alive?" asked the astonished family.

"I knew I was in the path of duty, so I prayed to God to keep me and walked straight on. The wild dogs snapped at me, but did not touch me," was Andrew's calm reply.

This was a pastor whose love for people was undaunted, and not to be taken lightly!

Amazingly, it was a love that would soon take an extraordinary new step in ministry.

5

Vacations Beyond the Vaal

P astor Murray, tell us please of your trip. We are all here because we are anxious to hear of your time with our friends in the Transvaal."

Andrew was still road-weary and ill. He had just returned from a "vacation" beyond the Vaal River, six weeks of hard travel and ministry. He was now seated with the elders, the consistory of the church in Bloemfontein, and they wanted to know how God had blessed this bold venture by the young pastor they were growing to love more and more.

"Well, I knew our last encampment was going to be quite large. On Monday following Sabbath the *Raad* (Boer Parliament) was scheduled to meet, so large numbers of people had already begun to gather."

"How many would you guess were present, sir?" asked one elder, leaning forward.

"That is hard for me to say exactly. I was told that there were about four hundred wagons brought 'round. A very large place for meeting had been prepared with seating for at least one thousand. Still it was too small by half I would say. I had preached already on Friday and twice on Saturday as people were still arriving. There were as well many other things to see to. Baptisms and weddings. We were also examining people for membership.

"Still, I was unprepared for the crowd when I stepped into the pulpit to prepare for communion on Sunday. All I could see was a vast sea of souls, people for whom Jesus gave His life. What had I to give so many?

"I preached as best I could, trying to set forth as faithfully as I could what Psalm 24:4 shows us of the way to God. There David instructs us as to God's requirements for ascending to His presence. He writes: 'the one who has clean hands and a pure heart, who does not lift up his soul to an idol, or swear by what is false.'

"I remember my own heart being touched as I spoke on Emmanuel, 'God with us,' as God's own way for our hearts to be pure. Yet I fear few of the people were in a place in their own souls to understand that."

"What do you mean by that, Mr. Murray?" came the question.

"I mean that I could sense that many of the people simply expected to be scolded by the law of God. It was as if they actually wanted it. Take the lashes and go on with life. Of course, if scolding would produce godly effects, I would gladly scold them. But sometimes I feel sad at the thought that the blessed Gospel of God's love should be degraded to be nothing else than a schoolmaster to drive and threaten. I must say, I fear for the whole vision of God's love and the power of His grace among our people."

There was a quiet nod of agreement among the

church leaders. Many could easily remember, just a few months ago, how they too knew little of God's grace. This young minister, already deep in the things of God, had raised their vision well beyond "scolding" as he so aptly put it.

"And so, Reverend Murray, was that the end of the weekend?" The question brought everyone's attention back to the table.

"Oh, not at all. On Monday I preached on 1 John 4:7—'Dear friends, let us love one another, for love comes from God. Everyone who loves has been born of God and knows God.' I tried to speak as clearly as possible on all the contention and enmity that prevails among those who were gathered. It was plain to see. All one has to do is mention the *Raad* and tempers flare.

"That evening I had another opportunity to speak strongly on the same subject in the final sermon. My text was Philippians 1:27—'Whatever happens, conduct yourselves in a manner worthy of the gospel of Christ. Then, whether I come and see you or only hear about you in my absence, I will know that you stand firm in one spirit, contending as one man for the faith of the gospel.' I was exhausted, but there was given to me great strength from on high, both in body and in spirit. The service began about ten o'clock that evening, and we did not finish until past midnight, about two o'clock in the morning."

One could not be sure what to make of the quiet, reflective nods from these Boer elders as they listened to the report of their pastor. Certainly, there was thanks to God for His gracious work among their far-removed countrymen. There was no doubt a great sense of awe at the untiring passion of Andrew Murray to reach out with the Gospel of God's love.

The stage for this fascinating time in Andrew's ministry had been set years before his arrival in Bloemfontein. During and after the *Great Trek* some 7,000 of the sturdy Boer people had moved beyond even the wilds of the Orange River Sovereignty into territory referred to as the Transvaal, well past the reach of British control.

These large farm families led an isolated, semi-nomadic existence of hard work and rugged independence. There was no opportunity for formal education or corporate church life. They simply carried a conservative Dutch faith and a Bible with them wherever they went. There was also great suspicion of anything or anyone related to the British government, including, perhaps especially, ministers of the Dutch Reformed Church. These ministers were appointed and paid by the British governor, so their allegiance was more than suspect.

Andrew's heart must have been deeply moved as he learned more of their condition. Over the years, only a few missionary visitations had been made among the people. Bloemfontein was the nearest church to their territory, but ministry among them was not part of his charge. He was restricted in his official capacity to his own 50,000 square-mile parish. Unless he was on vacation!

Even before his first anniversary in Bloemfontein, Andrew decided to take his six-weeks holiday to pay a visit to the Boers beyond the Vaal. Arrangements were quickly made and a deacon was enlisted to join him.

They set off together, crossing the river on December 7, 1849, returning home on January 22, 1850. Sadly, upon their return, Deacon Coetzee died of what was presumed to be Delagoa Bay fever, which both men had contracted on the trip.

The men had covered more than 800 miles, usually by slow-moving ox wagon. Andrew's careful records show that he preached at six different stations, conducting thirty-seven formal services. Incredibly, he baptized 567 children and confirmed to membership 167 young people, less than half the number of candidates that applied.

Andrew would make two additional tours through the Transvaal during his time at Bloemfontein. Indeed, the Boers quickly looked to him as their pastor and regularly petitioned the governor to release him from Bloemfontein and assign him to their territory. These ventures were of enormous impact in many ways. Many lives were touched for Christ. Andrew's tour did much to draw the Boers together as a people, and to allay their suspicions toward the church. Most of all, it knit their hearts together in support of their ardent young pastor.

Such efforts were mightily used of God to spread the Gospel and its effects throughout the region. They also endeared Andrew to his people and built a level of trust that made him a leading citizen. So much so that when another great impasse with the British government emerged, Andrew was asked to travel to England to represent the interests of the people before the crown.

It seems that by mid–1853, the British governance of the Orange River Sovereignty had become so disjointed and ineffective that they faced a watershed moment. As colonists continued to settle and develop the area, tensions with the Boers continued unabated. At the same time, the conclusion of hostilities with the powerful African tribal groups known as the Eighth Kaffir War, by far the bloodiest and most costly to date, was barely holding. The British must either reinforce their hold on the area or abandon it. Just as they unilaterally chose to exert Sovereignty in 1848, so now, only five years later, they unilaterally chose to abandon the territory!

Needless to say, there was a great outcry against such a move from the residents of the area. English colonists had invested their lives and capital. Missionaries viewed the abandonment with dismay. Even a large number of Boer settlers felt the British ought to at least establish a measure of order before summarily leaving.

At a late summer gathering in Bloemfontein, meeting in the newly completed church structure, matters came to a head. Sir George Clerk, the British administrator charged with implementing a transfer of government, began the process of abandonment without even considering other options. The local delegates still chose to protest the action in hopes of putting a halt to it. Andrew and a retired army surgeon who had settled in the area were chosen to travel to England to represent the cause of the colonists.

Andrew considered the appointment with mixed feelings. Certainly, he felt constrained by his pastoral commitments from going, but representing his people in this matter would be a great service, and was clearly their own desire. There was his health to be considered: his pastoral schedule, visitation travels, community involvement, and missions beyond the Vaal River had clearly taken their toll on his physical well-being. Eventually it was decided that a change of climate and schedule would do him good.

Andrew accepted the charge and set off for London on the steamer *Queen of the South* on January 21, 1854. They arrived in late February and proceeded to pursue their case before the necessary officials.

Even as they were at work, events transpired back home in South Africa that left Andrew's mission incapacitated. A surge of Boer nationalism rose up and, to the great delight of Sir Clerk, laid claim to the opportunity for independence from British rule. The short-lived Orange River Sovereignty now became a Boer republic called the Orange Free State. Andrew's mission was for naught.

The time and travel were far from wasted. Andrew took the opportunity to visit Scotland and Holland. He passed through Germany as well, all the time seeking potential candidates for the ministry in South Africa. He intended to recruit pastors in much the same way that his own father had been brought to South Africa, though without success. He did have opportunity to preach often, sometimes to congregations as large as 3,000 people. These times of ministry he found to be refreshing. Andrew's ministry was well received on each occasion. A prominent London church even offered him an interim pastoral position.

His health, though, showed little improvement. Andrew reported his condition in letters home to his family:

> I feel my strength so worn that I do not believe that even perfect rest for three or four months would restore me, and a single summer in Africa would lay me prostrate. The doctor says that my whole system has been much more seriously affected than I have any idea of, and that prolonged rest is necessary to restoration. He advises that I should not leave before winter. . . . What I chiefly suffer from is the pain in my hands and arms. Half an hour's lively conversation, or earnest application to anything that requires thinking, immediately makes itself felt there. I cannot even write a note without feeling the pain in my arms. . . .

Andrew would draw things to a close in Europe and begin the journey home on March 9, 1855, arriving in South Africa in late May. He would not arrive back in Bloemfontein until August of that year, an absence of fully one year and nine months. His travel between Cape Town and Bloemfontein, by way of Graaf-Reinet, was delayed. It seems he found reason to hold over for several weeks in Cape Town.

6

A New Page in Life: Marriage and Family

Dinner guests were not an unusual occurrence in the house of Mr. Howson Rutherfoord, so one would expect little of note this night. Little except that their guest would be the fiery young preacher from Bloemfontein, Reverend Andrew Murray, who was just returning from England.

We can only look back and surmise that, indeed, something of note did take place that night, for before he left several weeks later for Bloemfontein, Andrew had become a regular dinner guest at the Rutherfoord home. He would also propose marriage to Mr. Rutherfoord's daughter, Emma. By all accounts it was love at first sight.

The Rutherfoord family had moved to South Africa from England. Mr. Rutherfoord did well as a merchant, and soon the family members were leading citizens of the colony. As an earnest Christian layman, Mr. Rutherfoord had committed his businesses to God's work, using them to underwrite many Christian causes. He was personally involved in a number of missions enterprises, as well as the

"Cape of Good Hope Society," which aided slaves in the purchase of their freedom. The entire family was active in the Church of England, and very generous in hospitality to missionaries and ministers of all denominations.

When Andrew arrived at their table, they were all taken by his broad range of experiences and cultural interests. They concluded that he was "a good talker, but always ready to listen."

Emma was twenty years old when Andrew first dined at her father's home. She declined his first proposal, but began a regular correspondence with him when he returned to Bloemfontein.

Born and raised in Cape Town, Emma was schooled in all the virtues and skills of a Victorian lady. She proved adept at music, art, languages, and the details of managing an extended household. In addition, she was widely read due to the encouragement and oversight of her mother. All these things would come to bear great fruit in her marriage to Andrew.

Andrew returned to Cape Town barely a year after first meeting Emma, and they were to be married on July 2, 1856. Andrew was twenty-eight years old, and Emma twenty-one.

Andrew chuckled quietly to himself as he observed his mother-in-law to be, busy and worrying with all the details of the upcoming wedding.

"Oh, Reverend Murray," she addressed him formally. The family still had more respect for this young Dutch minister than familiarity as a son-in-law. "How will we ever make arrangements for all the gifts and furnishings? It is just not right for a poor bride to start her married life without the traditional 'twelve dozen of everything!' What kind of mother will I appear to be!"

"Mrs. Rutherfoord, please," Andrew spoke with reassurance. "The Bloemfontein parsonage is fully stocked for living. You know that we are simply anxious to be married. As it is, we must already make provision for the transport of Emma's china and her piano. Imagine that, if you will! A piano in an ox wagon trekking out to the Orange Free State!"

Andrew could only be amused, for he was in love. More than in love—Andrew could sense that he had met God's special provision in his life. More than either could have possibly imagined, this was a match made in heaven.

"There, that settles it," said Mr. Rutherfoord with an obvious sense of relief. "The ceremony will be performed by Reverend Murray's uncle, Reverend Mr. Stegmann of the Lutheran Church of Cape Town. We will hold it at the Dutch Reformed Church in nearby Wynberg." This ecumenical compromise settled the delicate question of how to join a Dutch Reformed groom with a Church of England bride in an acceptable fashion.

The two enjoyed a "covered-wagon honeymoon" as they headed off for Bloemfontein. Emma's letters home spoke of her wonderment at the South African wilderness—the wide-open places and new sights. Nights spent out in the open thrilled her as "real pioneering." She was struck by the large Dutch families and their new customs.

They often sing a hymn in the middle of the sermon to wake the people up! I thought it was time to leave, and prepared to do so, when they all sat down again and continued! . . . I never saw such a marrying and children-loving people. If you want to get to their hearts, just admire the babies or talk to the children. My husband is very good at both; he understands quieting a baby far better than I do, but then he has even now a little sister of six months and has always had some little brother or sister to play with.

One thing Emma had not mastered by the time of their marriage was the Dutch language. But she would quickly learn, and quickly learn to love the people as well. Though she did not bend to the people's vision of the domestic wife, Emma was a partner to Andrew, a true helpmate.

Through the course of their married life, Emma saw to it that Andrew had the time and place of peace for recuperation from the demands of his ministry. As a bachelor pastor, Andrew had maintained an "open-door" policy with his people. Parishioners would come and go, in and out of the house at will. Counsel and prayer, discussion and teaching seemed to flow naturally throughout the day. Emma quickly adjusted to this and carried on the same sort of openness wherever they lived. She maintained order and stability in the house, even while he was often called to travel for long stretches of time. When Grey College was opened in Bloemfontein, shortly after the arrival of the newlyweds, their home was graciously opened for boarding students. This continued to mark their lifestyle for years to come.

Dr. Fredrick Kolbe spoke quietly, his mind

drawn back to those formative years in his own life, when as a student in Cape Town, he had a chance to board with the Murray family:

Yes, indeed. And quite a blessing it was. I hope that Mr. and Mrs. Murray knew by instinct how I loved them, though I could never bring myself to speak openly of it. I tell you this, if either of them had asked me to put my hand in the fire for them, I would have done it in an instant. Those years were a time I saw Reverend Murray at the closest possible quarters. And believe me, I may be shy, but I was not unobservant! Reverend Murray himself was a very highly strung man. Always bustling with nervous energy that just could not be contained. His preaching was so enthusiastic, his gesticulation so unrestrained, that he was wearing himself out. Or so several doctors felt.

Now, you might think that such an output of nervous energy might well mean some reaction at home. You would almost expect some kind of irritation with his wife, some unevenness with his children or a sharp word toward those of us in his house. For all of my time there, I cannot recall a single instance when he was thrown off balance or anything short of gracious, kind, and attentive. His harmony with Mrs. Murray would be understandable. She was such a gracious, wifely, motherly person, that not to be in harmony with her would itself be self-condemnation. And he never condemned himself on that score. Reverend Murray was solid gold all through.

Together, Andrew and Emma raised eight children who survived to adulthood, four sons and four daughters.

Their eldest son, Howson Rutherfoord, was named after Emma's father. A committed Christian, he entered business in Cape Town with his uncle, only to die suddenly at the age of twenty-three.

Emmie, their eldest daughter, served with the Salvation Army in Cape Town and rose to the rank of staff-captain. She later relinquished her connection with that organization to become director of Magdalena House, a Christian shelter ministry to young girls and women.

Mary, the second daughter, entered the mission field, working mainly among African tribal people. Kitty devoted her life to educational work, teaching, and administrating at several places, including the Branch Huguenot Seminary in Bethlehem, South Africa.

For the last twenty years of Andrew's life, their youngest daughter, Annie, served as personal secretary to her father. It was to Annie that he dictated most of his later works. We owe much to her for her part in Andrew Murray's writings.

Their second son, Andrew Haldane, studied at Christ's College in Cambridge before returning to South Africa to receive his M.A. degree. After some years of teaching he was appointed an inspector of schools. This he pursued diligently until deciding to settle into farming in the Graaf-Reinet district. He met an untimely death in 1916 in military service in East Africa related to World War I.

The Murrays had two sons who became missionaries. John served among the Basuto people in northern Transvaal. His brother Charles worked among the tribal natives in Nyasaland until his wife's poor health required a move to a more temperate climate.

Over the years, Emma was involved in the ministry. Tireless in her ongoing efforts with Sunday schools, she was also not one to miss new opportunities. She began a prayer meeting for women in the midst of the Worcester Revivals that continued in strength for decades. She developed creative ways to involve children in providing support for missionary needs. Many of the schools that were to flourish under Andrew's ministry owe much to her concern and care.

When their children were older, she often accompanied Andrew on his travels. Always, Emma acted as his sounding board for sermon ideas and evaluation. Her sharp mind could often relate Andrew's ideas to their sources in the books that they read aloud together. She was there for many of the most decisive times in Andrew's life: the revival in Worcester, the battles with liberalism in Cape Town, the silent years and his healing, his travel and, most of all, his writings. She was a constant companion and source of encouragement.

7

Revival!

In 1860, some four years after their marriage, Andrew and Emma moved with their two children to Worcester. It was a pleasant place, and different from Bloemfontein in many ways. For one thing the new parish was much smaller geographically. Andrew would have ministerial colleagues within thirty miles! Well-watered by the Hex River, Worcester was located on a broad plain and surrounded by lofty blue mountains. The diligent Dutch farmers of Worcester raised their crops just a few minutes' wagon ride from their neighbors, whereas the ranchers of Bloemfontein often lived in relative isolation on tracts of land that were many thousands of acres in size. This afforded better education for the citizens and their children, and a much closer sense of community.

In 1824, shortly after the village was founded, the church in Worcester had been established. Andrew's predecessor, Reverend Henry Sutherland, was a Scotsman who had come to South Africa at the instigation of Dr. Thom, just as Andrew's father had. He was a man of great prayer who served the people of Worcester for thirty-five years with devotion and piety. He often confessed that he was better at prayer than preaching, understandable since he never mastered the Dutch language. All the same, a number of people had an earnest faith, even if it was somewhat formal in expression. For years before Andrew's arrival, a humble group of intercessors had worn a small footpath to a hilltop looking out over the village from where they prayed for the people.

Andrew was installed as pastor there on Pentecost Sunday, May 27, 1860. In what now seems a prophetic beginning, his first sermon was preached from the text of 2 Corinthians 3:8—"Will not the ministry of the Spirit be even more glorious?"

Just a few months before the Murrays' arrival, the church in Worcester had been the site for a conference of Dutch Reformed ministers. The first of its kind in South Africa, the conference had caused a stir of interest and discussed a wide range of topics. Missions, the revivals taking place in the United States, and education had all been earnestly considered. Andrew had spoken fervently on the need to actively seek additional ministers for the South African churches.

———

"Reverend Murray! Reverend Murray! Come quickly, please, sir. There seems to be some kind of disturbance!" an elder of the Worcester Church called out for Andrew, who had just completed a service in English in the sanctuary. The poor man came running from another part of the church. He had the wild-eyed look of someone who just had come from the scene of a disaster.

"A disturbance?" asked Andrew, "what can this be?" Andrew broke into a run to keep up with the elder, who had turned on his heels and headed back. Andrew had been the pastor at the church in Worcester for only a few months, and he could not bear to think of things getting off on the wrong foot.

"It's the young people!" cried the elder. "You must come and see! I'm not sure what is happening or why, but there is an unbelievable commotion."

Andrew entered the room and stopped short. He could hardly believe his eyes and ears! Never had he experienced anything like the tumult that surrounded him. All around him the young people of his congregation were lost in prayer and praise to God. There were nearly sixty people in the room, and since most were praying out loud, the noise was deafening. No one seemed to notice the arrival of their esteemed pastor. Indeed, no one seemed to be aware of anyone else in the room. All seemed completely enthralled by an unseen presence. It was an overwhelming moment.

Suddenly regaining his focus, Andrew set about to discover exactly what was going on. Tentatively, he moved to the front of the meeting hall where he found the layman in charge of the meeting, Mr. deVries, kneeling in prayer. Andrew made his presence known several times, touching the man's shoulder and waiting. Shortly, Mr. deVries was roused from his prayer and rose to speak with his pastor.

"Mr. de Vries, are you not in charge here, sir?" queried Andrew.

"Well, yes, sir, I am. I suppose I am. At least I called the meeting to order. I mean, sir, that . . .

well, yes, sir, of course, sir, I am in charge." The stammering of Mr. deVries was respectful, though it made clear that the poor man was himself somewhat surprised by the goings-on. As Mr. deVries was an earnest and faithful layman, Andrew had every reason to trust his judgment. Yet, what was anyone to make of the situation?

"Mr. deVries, sir," Andrew spoke respectfully, but firmly, "how did this commotion happen upon us?" Clearly, he wanted an answer.

"Well, sir, it happened like this: We were gathered here this evening, and much as we have always done I began by leading the group in a hymn and a lesson from God's Word. Nothing unusual at all, sir! Oh yes, and then I prayed, just as I always do after the lesson.

"We then began to share hymn verses as we always do. Three or four young people would in turn give out a hymn verse. We would join them in song, and then they each prayed. It was then that a young colored girl (the South African term for a person of mixed racial heritage) rose from the back of the hall and asked if she too might propose a hymn.

"She is young, about fifteen years old, and works for a nearby farmer. I could introduce you to her if you like. She asked, and, well, sir, I hesitated at first, not knowing how such a thing would be received by those present. Better thoughts prevailed, sir, and I replied, 'Yes, of course! What would you have us to sing?'

"Well, sir, she led us in a verse. I am not even sure I remember exactly what, but I remember that she prayed. Or better, I remember *how* she prayed.

Quite moving, sir. Clearly, she was no stranger to conversation with God.

"It was while she was praying that we first heard the sound. First, quite faint and in the distance, but soon drawing nearer and nearer, until the very hall itself seemed to be shaken. It was amazing, sir! I hardly know what to make of it! Everyone seemed moved to prayer. With one or two exceptions, people dropped to their knees and began to pray audibly, though some only whispered. That is what happened, sir, and it has been just like that to this very moment!"

Andrew stepped back to ponder all that had been related. Beside him, Mr. deVries quietly dropped to his knees. He would later write in his personal account of these events: "It seemed to me that if the Lord was coming to bless us, I should not be upon my feet, but upon my knees."

The moment seemed to call Andrew to action. Decisively, he stepped forward and called out loudly, "People, silence!" Not a thing changed.

Again, he called out loudly, "People, I am your minister, sent from God! Silence!" If anyone heard his voice above the din, no one responded. There was simply no stopping the noise. All continued to pray and call on God for mercy and pardon.

Undaunted, Andrew turned back to Mr. deVries, rousing the man to his feet. At Andrew's request, the two began to sing the verse of a well-known hymn: "Aid the soul that helpless cries . . ." With good-hearted cooperation, Mr. deVries complied, but the two men were never more than a duet. Everyone went right on praying. Andrew was now quite flustered. What was happening to his people?

What was he to make of this unexpected outburst? Why would they not respond to his authority and leadership?

With what dignity he had left, Andrew prepared to depart from the hall. Stopping just at the back door, he turned for one last exclamation. "God is a God of order, and here everything is confusion!" With that, he turned and left.

So began the Great Revival of 1860. Andrew's father had prayed each Friday night for more than thirty years for such a fresh visitation of God, and Worcester had just recently been the site of a minister's conference that discussed revival. Andrew would one day be identified with revival movements such as this worldwide. At the moment that an actual visitation of God first occurred, Andrew not only nearly missed it, he resisted it!

Why was Andrew's initial response to this first outpouring so skeptical? Was it just the noise and apparent disorder that troubled him? Certainly, Andrew was no stranger to heartfelt expressions of faith. His passionate heart and fiery preaching were known across South Africa as antidotes to the typically formal and unemotional style of Dutch Reformed church life. Was it the apparent spontaneity of the event, occurring even without the formal preaching of the Word? Whatever his reasons were for resisting this move at first, clearly this was a turning point in the life and ministry of Andrew Murray. He was a different man by the time the revival subsided.

Mr. deVries went on to become a minister in the Dutch Reformed Church and is our best resource concerning this fascinating point in Andrew's life.

Nearly forty years later, Mr. deVries described the events following that first night:

> After that, the prayer meetings were held every evening. At the commencement there was generally great silence, but after the second or third prayer the whole hall was moved as before, and everyone fell to praying. Sometimes the gathering continued till three in the morning. And even then many wished to remain longer, or returning homeward, went singing through the streets. The little hall was soon quite too small, and we were compelled to move to the school building, which also was presently full to overflowing, as scores and hundreds of country folk streamed into the village.
>
> On the first Saturday evening in the larger meeting house, Mr. Murray was the leader. He read a portion of Scripture, made a few observations on it, engaged in prayer, and then gave others the opportunity to pray. During the prayer which followed on his, I heard again the sound in the distance. It drew nearer and nearer, and suddenly the whole gathering was praying.
>
> That evening a stranger had been standing at the door from the commencement, watching the proceedings. Mr. Murray descended from the platform and moved up and down among the people, trying to quiet them. The stranger then tiptoed forward from his position at the door, touched Mr. Murray gently, and said in English: "I think you are the minister of this congregation: be careful what you do, for it is the Spirit of God that is at work here. I have

just come from America, and this is precisely
what I witnessed there.

Before long, Andrew had become a thorough-
going supporter of the revival that was now spreading throughout the Dutch Reformed Church of
South Africa. Reports of similar occurrences from
other congregations began to pour in. Revival
seemed to break out first among those congregations that were represented at the Worcester Conference of the previous April, though even churches
that were without a pastor at the time were drawn
into this mighty move of God.

Wonderfully, the revival did not seem limited to
any single group or section. Churches in towns and
villages were touched, just as individuals and families in the most isolated rural areas experienced
the same renewing. Andrew traveled over the next
year to other places like Graaf-Reinet and Cape
Town disseminating the seeds of revival.

Of course, this revival had its excesses and de-
tractors. It seems every authentic work of God has
both. However, the mark of any true revival is the
fruit of lives changed by God, not the presence or
absence of problems. Testimonies of significant
change from this time abound.

Records show that a weekly prayer meeting had
been attempted in a section of the Worcester parish
just months before the revival. At first, so little interest was shown that attendance remained at
three or four brave souls. At the height of the revival, people flocked to prayer meetings all across
the district. People of every age and station in life,
without distinction of color, would gather not

weekly, but daily, even three times a day, and complain only when the meeting ended too soon! In the years that followed, fifty young men offered themselves for the ministry of the Word (from Worcester alone!), when previously it had been almost impossible to find men for the work.

Professor Hofmeyer of the Stellenbosch Seminary in South Africa records this story:

> There is a farmer whom I have known for years, a man of quiet and retiring disposition, who in company takes but little part in the general conversation. Two or three weeks ago he was suddenly seized with a feeling of terror when he thought of his sins. For a few days he was subject to a most violent inward struggle, which ended in a joyous and promising conversion. Shortly afterward he was visited by some of his friends who knew nothing of the change of heart that he had undergone. They were greatly moved when this silent man began to speak to them, in deeply earnest manner and with searching look, of the old truths that through the enlightenment of the Holy Spirit had become new to him.

Similarly, the consistory of the church in Wellington would record in its report to the presbytery that "the parish had made greater moral and spiritual progress in the last few weeks than in the whole course of its history since its establishment." In a letter to his wife, a member of the South African parliament wrote about his visit to the town of Calvinia after revival had swept through. He said that he could find no words to express the marvelous change that had come over the inhabitants since his visit in the previous year.

Finally, the words of Andrew Murray, Sr., who came to visit his son and observe the outpouring shortly after it began in Worcester: "Andrew, my son, I have longed for such times as these, which the Lord has let you have."

8

Battle for the Soul of the Church

R ight Reverend, sir!" Andrew Murray, Sr., addressed with great respect, as all did, the newly elected Moderator of the Synod of the Dutch Reformed Church of South Africa. The senior Murray's respect was tinged as well with pride and thankfulness as he spoke, because that Moderator was his own son Andrew.

Imagine! Though only thirty-four years old, Andrew had been elected Moderator of the Synod. It was a singular honor for a man so young to hold such an important position, but Andrew would be elected five additional times through the course of his ministry.

At this time, October 1862, the fruit of revival was still fresh in Andrew's congregation in Worcester. His family continued to grow and, as always, his interests ranged far and wide. Now, on top of it all, came the responsibility of the highest position in the entire South African church.

The Synod was the most important meeting in the life of the Dutch Reformed Church of South

Africa. Held only once every five years, it was a time
of renewed acquaintances, inspiration, and church
business. Fifty-three ministers from all across
southern Africa and even more elders had gathered
in Cape Town. Some traveled more than nine hundred miles by oxcart to make the meetings, and
would be gone from home for three months or more!
With his father, two brothers, and four brothers-in-
law all in attendance as ministers, it must have
seemed like a family reunion for Andrew.

This was a time for serious work and business
as well. Andrew's position as Moderator was not
just an honorary one. It involved more than simply
moving the Synod through its work in an orderly
way over the two months that it would be in session. Indeed, Andrew would find himself at the center of several major controversies; controversies
that would span several years, testing his capabil-
ities and convictions, even taking him into civil
court.

The first flash point of controversy at the Synod
revolved around the question of just who was and
who was not a legitimate voting delegate to the
Synod. It seems that the Dutch Reformed Church
had continually extended its ministry to the Dutch
settlers who moved farther and farther inland to escape the jurisdiction of the British crown ruling
South Africa. As a result of that missionary work,
a number of churches resided outside the boundaries of the colony of South Africa. Even Andrew took
"vacation mission trips" to the frontier sections of
the Transvaal while he was the pastor at Bloemfontein.

But the Dutch Reformed Church was an established State Church. It drew power and legal authority from its recognized position and official connection with the state. This set the stage and now, at this meeting of the Synod, controversy erupted regarding the status of those ministers and elders from churches that were outside the boundaries of the Colony. The churches in question were clearly Dutch Reformed in origin and practice. But their members were not citizens of South Africa. Could they really be voting delegates to a Synod of a State Church, even when they were not citizens of the state?

At first, the Synod ruled that these delegates were acceptable voting members at the meeting. In response, a lawsuit was filed in civil court against the decision by several members of the Synod. After the Synod adjourned, pastors and elders made the long trip home and resumed their work.

It was April 1863 when the decision of the courts was returned. To Andrew's dismay, they ruled against the Church! The Court reasoned that the agreement that had established the Dutch Reformed Church as the State Church of South Africa, the Church Ordinance of 1843, required that members of the church be citizens of the state as well. Ministers and elders from churches outside the national boundaries were not eligible to vote in the Synod.

The Synod was called back into session later that year. There had been one unfinished matter from the previous year that must now be attended to. Underlying the contention over church government was another, much more critical disagreement that had to do with theology and belief.

Since Andrew's time in Holland, liberalism had taken sway over the Church to a large degree. It now completely dominated the hearts and minds of ministers and church people there. By this time, it had even begun to affect life in the more conservative Dutch Reformed Church of South Africa. At the 1862 Synod, lengthy debate ensued regarding the allegiance of ministers to the Heidelberg Catechism.

This statement of Christian faith was written in 1563, a fruit of the Reformation that swept through Europe in the sixteenth century. It had been, and continues even today, to be the most important statement of faith among the Dutch-speaking Reformed churches around the world. The Catechism is clearly Reformed in its perspective, organized in three divisions: "The Misery of Man," "The Redemption of Man," and "Thankfulness." Of the many Reformed Catechisms, this is the one most noted for its warmhearted pastoral style. The first question, "What is your only comfort in life and in death?" is met with the profound response that follows: "That I with body and soul belong to my faithful Savior Jesus Christ."

Officially, the Dutch Reformed Church held that the Heidelberg Catechism was to be accepted by all of its ministers and elders *because* its statements were consistent with the Scripture. In addition, pastors were required to teach through the entire Catechism each year to ensure that every church was presented with the full scope of Christian belief.

At the 1862 Synod, that traditional position had come under attack by the "modernist" party, led by

Reverend J. J. Kotze, pastor of the church in Darling. He rose and protested a particular section of the Catechism—question sixty, which declared that humanity is "continually inclined to all evil." Reverend Kotze declared to the Synod that such a statement "would not be fitting in the mouth of a heathen—unless he was a devil—far less in the mouth of a Christian." He went on to say that if he ever did refer to that section in his ministry, he would do as a minister in Holland did, and simply say, "I believe that the Catechism is here in error."

It was an electric moment as the Synod now reconvened in 1863. Years of underlying tensions now rose to the surface and divided the group into two opposing parties. Battle lines were drawn, and any astute observer could look over the crowd and see the "moderns" and "orthodox" often sitting side by side.

At that moment, neither side would give in, though soon the tide would turn, leaving many to pursue ministry elsewhere. Many of the "moderns" were clergy, and made much of their learning. In the commotion, however, there was little chance to actually examine the depth of their knowledge or conviction. Few elders would align themselves with the "moderns," and so it was that the orthodox party had a bare majority.

The fuse of an explosive situation was lit when the Synod voted 56 to 24 to suspend Reverend Kotze from his ministerial duties because of his unacceptable theological views. Further, if he did not retract his divergent views within the next year, the Synod's representative committee was to discharge him from the ministry altogether when it met in 1864. Amidst a hushed silence, Andrew rose to speak to the gathered assembly.

"If there was a moment when I could have desire that another were occupying my place, it is now." In Andrew's voice there was a gravity that held the assembly in silence.

"We must now proceed to fulfill a solemn duty— a task which has never been undertaken in the Church of South Africa. After long and prayerful consideration, this Synod has concluded that one of the brethren has been guilty of holding false doctrine. He has been unfaithful to the solemn promise he made at his ordination. Having been found guilty, he may no longer fulfill the sacred office of pastor."

There was no joy of victory in Andrew's words. He was more concerned with a brother lost than a battle won.

"This is not the conclusion of the matter, however," he continued, "for it remains the Christian duty of each of us to offer earnest and continual prayer that the Lord might convince this erring brother of his error, and give him a heart of repentance.

"Even more, in this solemn hour, each of us ought to humble ourselves before the Almighty and remember the words of the apostle Paul, 'If you think you are standing firm, be careful that you don't fall' (1 Corinthians 10:12)."

With that, Andrew bowed his head and led the assembly in prayer.

Everyone realized that the vote to release the modernist leader could only pass when the votes of those ministers and elders from outside of South

Africa were included. Over the course of the ensuing year, the minister and his church in Darling refused to accept the decision of the Synod. Reverend Kotze filed a lawsuit in the civil court to prevent the committee from enforcing the decision of the Synod.

Andrew, as Moderator, was named in the suit. As the case went to court in August of 1864, accusations and stories flew, both in the churches and the press. It was the leading topic of the day throughout the nation. To make things worse, the church's attorney was unable to appear because of sickness on the scheduled day of the court hearing. Andrew was left to make the church's case by himself. He spoke forcefully for nearly four and a half hours. Though the court commended Andrew's defense, when they published their decision on September 1, they ruled against the Church on the grounds of the same Church Ordinance of 1843.

Another round of the battle resumed with another case that had begun at the same Synod of 1862, but had dragged on in similar fashion. Also involved in this case were the views of Reverend T. F. Burgers. Burgers had gone even further than Kotze in his rejection of Christian belief by denying the existence of the devil, the sinlessness of Christ, the resurrection of the dead, and the continued existence of the soul after death.

Back on March 19, 1864, when the representative committee of the Synod was passing a final sentence on Kotze, they had also deliberated on the case of Reverend Burgers. The committee chose to conditionally suspend Burgers from his office as minister until he changed his views. Rather than change, he too took the Church to court, and once again Andrew, as Moderator, was called on to defend the decision of the Church. This case was heard by the court on May 26, 1865.

It was now some three years since Andrew had been elected Moderator. In the meantime, he had taken a new charge, leaving Worcester and becoming third minister of the *Groote Kerk* in Cape Town. One can imagine that by now, having been named in three lawsuits, Andrew could hardly consider the position of Moderator an honor. He felt deeply for the truth of Christian orthodoxy. No doubt the prayers of his father, the instruction in his uncle's Scottish home, and his own firmness as a student in Holland were all coming to fruition. He carried on with the issues of the Synod, standing firm and resolute for the historic faith of the church universal.

As Andrew presented the Church's case before the court, he argued passionately that the Church had spiritual authority over its own members, an authority that was outside the jurisdiction of a civil court. Once again, the matter was decided against the Church on the grounds of the Church Ordinance of 1843.

When the Synod's Committee met in April 1865, they realized much was at stake for the life of their church and so decided to appeal the court's decision by going to the personal representative of the Queen of England, the Privy Council. Andrew was appointed as part of the delegation to make the Church's appeal.

On May 14, Andrew, Emma, and their five children boarded a steamship for faraway London. They would be gone from South Africa for ten

months, during which time a sixth child, Andrew
Haldane (named, no doubt, in honor of Robert and
James Haldane, whose ministry in Switzerland
had so influenced Andrew while he was a student
in Holland) was born. Shortly after they arrived in
London, Andrew received the sad news of his father's death. In a letter home to his mother, Andrew
wrote:

> The news of our dear father's departure has
> just reached us. You will not think it strange if
> I say that I could not weep. I felt that there was
> too much cause for thanksgiving. How indeed
> can we thank God aright for such a father, who
> has left us such a precious legacy in a holy life
> so full of love to us and labor in his Master's
> work. May his example be doubly influential
> now that we have him glorified with His Savior.
> For he is still ours.

England must have been an enjoyable adventure for the family. Emma visited with relatives.
Andrew renewed acquaintances on excursions to
Scotland and Holland. He even had opportunity to
preach often, and in a variety of places from conferences to prisons.

One such event was on Christmas Day, when
Andrew preached in a prison. The captive audience
of nearly two hundred thieves was hardly in a mood
to listen, so they began to cough loudly, drowning
out his message. Taking out his watch, Andrew
spoke to the crowd and said, "One at a time, gen-
tlemen, one at a time. As the sailor said to the minister while his donkey brayed: 'Either you or the
donkey!' So I will give you five minutes to cough and

you will give me five minutes to preach." When Andrew's five minutes were up, the men were so taken with this new preacher from South Africa that they gladly held their coughing until he was done!

Unfortunately, the court case that was the reason for their journey did not go nearly as well. The Church lost its appeal, and so no longer had the power to suspend a minister whom it judged to be unorthodox.

As happy as Andrew would have been to arrive home in South Africa, it must surely have been a sad turn of events. Shortly after his return in 1867, the full Synod of the Church of South Africa met. Andrew stepped down from his long five-year term as its Moderator. The Church had been overruled by the civil courts. Reverends Kotze and Burgers were present in the meeting, undisciplined and unrepentant. The Synod found itself in a very uncomfortable position, and unable to effectively find relief.

But all was not lost. During the five years of controversy, church matters and issues of faith were widely discussed. Theological debates became headlines. People all across the country became aware of the inroads liberalism had made into the Church and the consequences that followed. God had, in a most unusual way, worked a renewing of convictions in the lives and hearts of many citizens.

For all the appearance of defeat, history shows that by the end of these five years, liberalism had effectively spent its energy, and, in the Dutch Reformed Church at least, was defeated. Reverend Kotze would continue to pastor the church in Darling, though with little influence elsewhere, until he retired. Reverend Burgers continued in his pastorate for only two more years, at which time he was elected President of the Transvaal and severed his ties with the Dutch Reformed Church completely. Of the other liberal ministers, some withdrew to other denominations more in sympathy with their views, while others returned to more orthodox convictions.

God was at work through Andrew's faithful service in his church. What first appeared to be controversy, distracting and interrupting the revival that began two years earlier, served, in retrospect, as a time of renewed commitment and cleansing throughout the entire church. Andrew's strength of conviction and humble compassion as he carried out the disciplinary actions of the Synod were unswerving. Indeed, as Andrew served faithfully, his stature and ministry continued to grow. One detractor wrote in a local newspaper that even at the height of the controversy he could still recognize in Andrew a worthy opponent:

> One of the men of the ultra-orthodox party, who pose as watchmen on the walls of Zion, is Reverend A. Murray—a worthy leader. Eloquent, quick, and talented, he has an acute mind and clear judgment. He instantly knows the weak points of his opponents' arguments and knows how to assail them. He carries the meeting with him; he is too clever for most. He understands the art of making his ideas so attractive to the elders and the small minds among the ministers (who all look up to him with reverence) that they very seldom venture

to contradict Demosthenes, or as another has called him, Apollos. It would be sacrilege to raise a voice against the Right Reverend, the Actuarius, Andrew Murray. There is no member of the Assembly who possesses more influence than he, and certainly no one among the conservatives who better deserves his influence. He is consistent, and consistency always demands respect.

9

The Cape Town Pastorate

T he 'ayes' have it," cried the Moderator at this
important meeting of the Dutch Reformed
Church in Cape Town. "The Reverend Andrew
Murray of Worcester shall be called to fill the va-
cancy occasioned by the recent retirement of Reverend J. Spijker!"

It was July 5, 1864, near the middle of Andrew's
term as Moderator of the Synod. Though still em-
broiled in the civil suits, he now received a call to
serve a joint pastorate at the church in Cape Town.
He wrote to his father, sharing his internal struggle
over whether to accept the call. All of his friends
from outside Worcester, as well as his own incli-
nations, pointed to Cape Town. Still, he wrestled intently. That one little word "yes" implied so much
in terms of commitment to a new task. In the end,
he would go to Cape Town, more out of surrender to
God's purpose for him than in any strength or conviction of his own. "If God wills to bless, no instru-
ment is too weak, and blessed it is to be the instru-
ment that He condescends to use."

Andrew was the first pastor in the two-hundred-
year history of the church to be called by a vote of

the congregation. All previous pastors had been appointed by the governor. Surely, this was one more sign of the changing relationship between the church and state in South Africa.

Cape Town was the first European settlement in what is now South Africa. In Andrew's day, as now, it was the largest city in the country and an important seat of government, commerce, and culture. The new call placed his life and ministry at the very heart of national life in South Africa.

The church was enormous for its day. A team of three ministers served the 3,000 members and 5,000 adherents. Each would preach one Sunday in rotation while sharing pastoral responsibilities.

Andrew saw great opportunity, and to the extent he was able with the lawsuits, gave his great energy to the work. He showed a particular interest in ministry to the youth. Reverend C. Rabie would look back on this time and write:

> I was one of those privileged to be confirmed by Mr. Murray. He always turned us to the Bible and made us read and explain all the answers. Every time the class was over, he asked two or three to remain and he had a personal talk with them about the condition of their souls. Many of us date our spiritual birth from those talks.

By 1865, Andrew had helped found and was elected president of the first YMCA in South Africa. He worked hard to see the success of this organization, which, in its origins, was thoroughly evangelical in perspective, often involved in social service and outreach to the unchurched.

He began English-speaking services at Cape Town's historic Dutch church, and two new week-night services for working people who were unable to attend on Sunday.

In this urban setting, Andrew was quick to recognize the needs of the poor. In church writings he spread the principles of the most progressive urban ministry and outreach, known then as "slum work," that were being developed in Edinburgh, Scotland. At his urging, new school buildings and programs were developed for the children of Cape Town's poor, soon encompassing nearly 1,000 children. In all that he did, he always recognized the supreme need for human redemption in Christ and for the loving involvement of the church, modeled on the incarnation of Christ. A portion of an article written by Andrew during this time illustrates his convictions well:

> Merely to build schools and churches for the poor is to offer them stones for bread. There must be living, loving Christian workers, who, like Elisha of old, will take the dead into their arms and prayerfully hold them close, until they come to life again.

Andrew's battle with liberalism was not restricted to the Dutch Reformed Church. He returned from England at one point to find all Cape Town ablaze with modernist talk. During his absence a portion of the congregation—out of some 3,000 members 527 had signed the document—had petitioned the governing board of the church, asking them to call as pastor none other than Reverend J. J. Kotze! Their petition read, in part, that "the choice of the minister mentioned will greatly contribute toward removing the estrangement which has for some time existed between the consistory (the church's governing board) and a large portion of the congregation." This request was not in accordance with church law, and so could not be honored. It does however show the kind of sentiment that this minority possessed.

In the end, the church called a cousin of Andrew's, Reverend G. W. Stegmann, as their third pastor, and a number of prominent members of the Cape Town Church withdrew to other congregations, most notably the new Free Protestant Church. The pastor there, Reverend David Faure, had recently returned from seminary training in Holland. Unable to find reception among the Dutch Reformed churches in South Africa, he assembled a congregation and began to preach. A series of thirteen of his lectures presenting the rationalistic theology of Dutch liberalism was soon published under the title *Modern Theology*.

Andrew took the challenge head on and preached a series of sermons both in Dutch and English that dealt topic for topic and argument for argument with Faure's book. When Andrew's series was published as *A Lecture on the Modern Theology*, Mr. Faure himself said "both as regards matter and manner Mr. Murray's lectures were far superior to others that responded to his book (*Modern Theology*) and they represent the only serious attempt made to meet argument with argument." The Cape Town newspaper reviewed Andrew's book and concluded that it was "keen in thought, scientific in treatment, and as profoundly philosophical in its essence as it was eloquent in expression."

Andrew was far more than an argumentative defender of the faith in his writing. It was in Cape Town that he began to invest more effort into writing the books that would become his greatest contribution to the generations that followed. Growing out of his ministry in Bloemfontein and Worcester, Andrew had already published a book in Dutch regarding children. We have it today with the title *How to Raise Your Children for Christ*. While at Cape Town he published several more works in Dutch, most notably a series of thirty-one meditations on Psalm 51 that was published in English as *Have Mercy Upon Me*.

His wife, Emma, was a constant companion and encouragement in his literary work. She did far more than care for their expanding family, which became five daughters (two of whom would die early and untimely deaths) and three sons by the time they left Cape Town. Her sewing machine was one of the first in Cape Town, and the children remember their family being the first to bring the game of croquet to South Africa.

Their home on Kloof Street was more than simply a place of refuge for Andrew from the controversies of the day. It was a warm place for their expansive ministry of hospitality. Students, missionaries, and others often found welcome and refreshment there.

Above all else though, Andrew understood himself to be a pastor—a man called to the care of souls. He carried on a vigorous visitation ministry, even in so large a congregation. During a severe smallpox epidemic, which claimed many victims in Cape

Town, Andrew was unafraid to visit and comfort the afflicted. He expressed frustration that in a church so large he could face an entire congregation of faces different from those he had just visited that week. How could he know and care for so large a group?

Eventually, in 1871, a call came from a smaller church in Wellington, some forty-five miles outside of Cape Town. To the surprise of many, Andrew took it. It seemed a step out from the sure rise to prominence that would come with the pastorate in Cape Town. It was a deep sense of pastoral calling and a yearning for quiet intimacy with God that tipped the balance in favor of Wellington, the place Andrew would serve for almost thirty-five years, and then retire to live out his days. As he put it in a letter to his brother:

> My first work, my calling, is to be a pastor; where I can be happy in this work, thither I feel myself drawn. I do think that I have honestly and in childlike simplicity said to the Father that if He would have me stay here, I am ready and willing. . . .

10

Bearing Fruit: The Wellington Pastorate

Reverend Murray stepping down from the great Cape Church! Preposterous! And that in order to settle in Wellington? Why would a minister of his prestige and future move from the most important congregation to such a little pastorate in a pasture? A few more years and he is sure to be Senior Minister here. Why would he want to leave?"

The year was 1871, and no doubt many people spoke these same thoughts. Andrew announced his decision to take the call as pastor of the Dutch Reformed Church in Wellington. It must have been a surprise to many.

Wellington was a country parish situated at the end of the rail line from Cape Town. It was an important commercial center. Goods and people going to and from Cape Town and the outlying areas all converged here.

The town numbered some 4,000 residents and was the center of a prosperous farming district. Surrounded on the south and east by rugged mountains that opened into fertile green valleys, Wellington was well fed by broad rivers flowing across the panorama in what was described by one visitor as "beauty in the lap of grandeur."

Was Andrew simply exhausted from the years of court battles in Cape Town? Was his health, strained since his first years in Bloemfontein, beginning to falter? Certainly, many thought this was the reason for his move.

"Why call Reverend Murray?" one old Wellington farmer was heard to ask. "In two years time we will have the expenses of another funeral."

Correspondence to his brother John, for some years now leading professor at the Stellenbosch Seminary in South Africa, reveals another conclusion. In Cape Town, Andrew missed the intimacy of personal pastoral work. Wellington gave him opportunity to preach to the same people week by week. He could visit those unable to attend regularly. He could baptize and catechize and minister in ways that were impossible in the urban setting. Here he could cultivate lives, even as his farmers cultivated their vineyards.

These vineyards would be the center of two fascinating events in his time at Wellington.

Apparently, the congregation was unaware, or had not taken seriously, Andrew's firmly held temperance convictions. Things could have come to a difficult impasse had it not been for Andrew's delicate care. Andrew gave the following analogy:

> When a farmer trains a young horse, it will often shy at a stone or something else. The wise farmer will quietly lead the horse to the unfa-

miliar object and let him look at it and smell it till all fear passes, and it will not shy anymore. So I will not force temperance upon you, but we will speak and preach about it till you are familiar with it and approve of it.

For all Andrew's gentleness, things did not go well for a time. His daughters remembered having to watch the parsonage carefully around the clock. Attempts were made to burn down the home with the Murray family inside. More than once, rags soaked in kerosene were hurled into windows. "God, in His great mercy, graciously protected us, but we exercised great care and watchfulness at this time."

Andrew persisted to hold his conviction for temperance *and* for love.

"Mr. Murray, the congregation will be torn asunder by your temperance sentiments," declared an angry wine producer one day.

"Never," declared Andrew without flinching. "We will, if necessary, take the scissors of love and cut it in two, having one section for temperance and the other not, but we will live together in love."

Over time, matters began to settle down, and with peace came the blessing brought about by Andrew's convictions. For most of Andrew's ministry, Wellington supported only four saloons, compared to more than forty during the same time in another nearby community of similar size.

God often uses controversy and trials as the raw material for a healthy pastoral relationship of love and respect. That must certainly have been the case for Andrew Murray and the Wellington congregation. Andrew would spend the rest of his life there, some forty-six years in all, thirty-five of them as their pastor.

Andrew also had things to learn from his farming congregation. As he watched them tend their vineyards, cultivating, pruning, and caring for them, Andrew gained insight into the words of Jesus in John 15. Watching them gave him insight into the Father and His purposes. Out of this observation came the book, *The True Vine*, a marvelous exposition of John 15 and the abiding life.

The Lord's Table is another book inspired by Andrew's experience during the Wellington pastorate.

"It is the communion services that I will never be able to forget." Annie Murray, Andrew's youngest daughter and for the final twenty years of his life his personal secretary, thought back over her life—so singularly contained here in Wellington.

"There around the Lord's Table, some 500 or 600 people would gather. There was a Holy Influence that seemed to hang in the air all around us. I could never forget the Holy Awe, the deep reverence, the joy written upon my father's face. It was as if he stood before us, but was carried beyond, to the very presence of Christ.

"I remember a particular time when Father seemed to have really been taken up to the third heaven and a holy awe and deep solemnity rested on us all before he spoke again. We waited, as if time had stopped. And then he spoke, 'I live, yet not I but Christ liveth in me, and that life which I now live in the flesh, I live in faith, the faith which is in the Son of God who loved me and gave himself for me.'

"He especially seemed to dwell on those words 'who loved me.'

"We left the table feeling that we had indeed been fed on heavenly manna, and we rose with deeper love, and fuller determination to do and dare all for our adorable Lord and Master. We were strengthened and refreshed as with new wine, and in the afternoon, the thanksgiving service was a time of wondrous praise, not from the lips alone, but from the heart."

Over the course of the years, Wellington would be a firm and supportive home base for Andrew's increasingly far-flung ministry. This was the place from which the majority of his books would flow. As has been mentioned, he served five times as Moderator of the Synod of the Dutch Reformed Church during his tenure as pastor. He took nine different evangelistic tours throughout the provinces of South Africa, and four trips overseas—including trips to the United States and to England's Keswick Convention.

Wellington became a base of prayer support for Andrew's increasingly wide-ranging ministry. He trained and inspired his people to see prayer as the key to entering into God's full purpose on earth. Once again, out of this specific pastoral experience came books, most notably *The Ministry of Intercession* and *The Prayer Life*.

Andrew's writing had begun years before he moved to Wellington. In 1858, he had published in Dutch *Jesus, the Children's Friend*. Interesting that a man who would come to be known for such profound spirituality would begin with a children's life of Jesus.

Andrew's second book, again in Dutch, was entitled *What Manner of Child Shall This Be?* It was a collection of meditations and baptism addresses he had given to believing parents as he traveled and ministered from Bloemfontein. Andrew would stop for a covered-wagon service in the Transvaal and often baptize fifty children at a time after personal examination of the parents. Later published in English as *How to Raise Your Children for Christ*, this book was to be a guide and study for those parents after he left.

Once settled into Wellington, books, tracts, and articles began to flow from his pen with increasing regularity. As many as 250 titles are known to be his, many translated into other languages, often even without his knowledge. A large number of tracts and articles in church magazines, while unsigned, bear his mark.

Because of pain in his arms and hands, he would regularly dictate to his wife, Emma. She was a good secretary and a ready sounding board for his ideas. After Emma's death, their youngest daughter, Annie, ably filled that same position; carefully taking notes, writing out the ideas and prose that flowed from her father's heart, always available to faithfully record his work.

11

Laborers for the Harvest

A ndrew, come to dinner, please," cried Emma, somewhat bewildered.

"Yes, of course, dear. I am right on the way." Andrew spoke automatically as he turned one more page in his book.

"Andrew, that is exactly what you said five minutes ago and then twice before that. I know you too well to wonder. What are you reading that has you so distracted?"

With that, Andrew surfaced from his deep concentration and prepared for the waiting dinner. Emma was right. He had found a book that absorbed him, given to him at the request of Emma by a friend of hers. They turned to it together when the evening meal was complete. He was reading *The Power of Christian Benevolence, Illustrated in the Life and Labors of Mary Lyon*. It would prove to be a watershed in his ministry.

Where the 1860s had been absorbed by the battle with liberalism, the 1870s were chiefly focused with the development of education in South Africa. This was an area of great importance to Andrew Murray.

A quality education was highly valued in Andrew's family—enough so that his parents had sent him and his brother John to Scotland for ten years. Andrew and Emma sent their daughters Emmie and Mary to the Moravian Institution at Zeist in Holland in 1872 in pursuit of training suitable to their potential.

Earlier, while in Bloemfontein, Andrew had been involved in the opening of Grey College, the second oldest institution of its kind in the Colony. The school was founded in 1856 for the purpose of training teachers. A large gift from the state treasury by the British governor at the time, Sir George Grey, made it all possible. Andrew had been immediately involved as a trustee and as rector overseeing boarding arrangements for the students as well as opening his own home for those students needing a home away from home.

Still, the need for education outstripped the opportunities. For years, Andrew had seen quality, Christ-centered education as a key to the future of South Africa. As early as 1859, in a letter to his brother John, he had seen that "Religious education must, I think, become the watchword of our church before we can expect abiding fruit on our labors . . . in the ordinary course of things, education is our hope."

It was Andrew's conviction that the best and proper source for Christian workers in South Africa was the Christian homes in South Africa itself. Who better to reach the peoples of this great continent than those who called it their home?

He constantly challenged parents to pray and encourage their children to give their lives in full-time service to the Kingdom of God. In 1872, Andrew began to write for the church paper advocating this very idea to the people of South Africa. In three memorable articles entitled "Our Children," he would refute, one by one, every conceivable argument that had parents holding back their children from God's service. The Lord had a right to our children, he maintained, and the Lord needed them as well. Lack of money for training or lack of special abilities by the child did not exempt them from the Lord's call. A parent's only child was not deferred from the call. Even our daughters, he declared, had a special place of service.

> The consecration of your daughters to God can never be a vain and idle matter. The Lord has latterly shown that He can use women to perform great and important services for His Church; and if parents only will present their daughters to the Lord, He will know how to prepare a sphere of work for them—as intercessors for others, as laborers in His Kingdom, in nursing the sick, or in caring for the poor.

Andrew went on to highlight a special capacity of service to the Lord, useful to both the Kingdom of God and the needs of South Africa: teachers! It is clear from the lives of his own children that he was simply sharing the convictions that motivated him and Emma in the raising of their own children.

Andrew found something new and striking in Mary Lyon and her institution, the Ladies Seminary in Mt. Holyoke, Massachusetts (known today simply as Mt. Holyoke College). He observed in Miss Lyon an insight that "was marvelously successful in rousing her pupils to aim enthusiastically at uniting the highest intellectual development with the most decided piety. First the Kingdom of God, but after that most certainly all science and knowledge."

The school was built upon two key principles: (1) It was to be thoroughly Christian in perspective. Trustees should have a view to the highest interests of the church of Christ and teachers should be inspired and able to inspire others with a missionary spirit. (2) The school should be simply and efficiently managed. Much of the work of running the institution was actually done by the students, rather than servants. This helped to keep fees low, making the school affordable to as many as wanted to attend, and prepared the young women for useful service of all sorts. He saw here a practical expression of the principles he had written about.

By 1873, things were beginning to take shape. Collections were taken. Construction was begun. First classes opened in June of that year. The church in Wellington was solidly behind the new work, helping in every way, including generous collections. Andrew wrote directly to Miss Lyon in Massachusetts, requesting that she recruit and send a suitable teacher. He personally guaranteed her salary. Miss Lyon obliged by sending *two* very capable women, Miss Hope and Miss Ferguson. They arrived in South Africa on November 16, and began a lifetime of fruitful service to the Kingdom of God and to South Africa.

January 1874 was the formal opening of the school in Wellington. It was given the name of the Huguenot Seminary—after those who had fled persecution in France and settled around the world, including Wellington. Over two thousand people came to the dedication services. Things were off to an amazing start. Best of all, within a short time, many of the students who had come without any faith would be "definitely won for Christ."

Space for forty boarders had been built already, but fifty-four applicants had been accepted from across South Africa. Expansion of facilities began almost immediately. For that cause Andrew began to travel widely on what he called "collection tours," first in 1874, and then for almost eight weeks in 1876. On this second tour, Andrew wrote home to Emma, saying,

> One thing has been very heavy on me all through . . . the idea of being on a mission for money, and having no time or opportunity to work for souls. . . . The thought suggests itself whether with such precious opportunities, so short and rare, it is right to preach a sermon for a collection. May the Lord direct and guide. We have said and do say that entire consecration to His work and will is our choice and our life. And we know that for all difficulties and questions that come we have an infallible solution in the assurance—Christ Who lives our life in us is sufficient for all that comes and will guide and keep us in perfect peace.

In the midst of the busy expansion of Huguenot Seminary, another opportunity came to Andrew that would be providential in its timing. In 1877, he would again be elected as Moderator of the Dutch

Reformed General Synod. Fortunately, there were no major controversies or civil suits to be handled as before. And with the position came another voyage to Europe and beyond.

12

Another Voyage

S o! This is Scotland," mused Reverend Charles
Murray, "land of our father's birth."

"Yes," answered his brother Andrew.
"Scotland. Where John and I came for our education. By God's grace that will never need be done again!"

As Moderator of the Dutch Reformed Church in South Africa, Andrew was made a delegate to the Pan-Presbyterian Council of 1877 held in Edinburgh, Scotland. His brother Charles, now pastor at Graaf-Reinet upon the retirement of their father, had been fortunate enough to accompany Andrew. Andrew's goal upon departure had been threefold:

(1) To study the condition of the church at large.
(2) To enquire into problems concerning education.
(3) To consider the spiritual life of the countries visited.

The Council was a worldwide gathering of representatives from the Presbyterian and Reformed churches scattered across the globe. For six days, 333 delegates, representing tens of thousands of ministers and congregations from around the world, met in the great cathedral of St. Giles.

The Council would prove to be an inspirational and outstanding gathering. Men like church historian Dr. Phillip Schaff, Dr. Alexander Hodge of Princeton, and Professor Frederic Godet of Switzerland would discourse on Christian unity, missions, ministering to the modern world, and the relationship between revelation and science. Andrew would address the Council on the importance of Christian education for young people. When all was said and done though, Andrew, with his keen sense of God's presence, would have an interesting reflection on the state of the church:

> When a large number of God's servants meet in order to consult about the interests of His Kingdom, and about the work they have to perform in connection with it, one would expect that their first felt need would be to place themselves as servants in the presence of their Lord, and while they wait there in worship and faith, to experience the renewal of those spiritual powers upon which everything depends. And yet it so frequently happens that in ecclesiastical and theological gatherings the so-called ordinary business occupies the first place, while hardly any time can be found for spiritual matters. And though we listened with great pleasure to what was said about the exercise of the spirit of love, about faithfulness to the doctrine of the Church, and about the earnestness displayed in the Council, more than one of us felt this great lack.

A whirlwind schedule kept Andrew and his brother on the go. Less than a week after the close of the Council, Andrew preached at a conference in nearby Iverness. From there the brothers traveled to Switzerland and Germany to pursue their three goals and to participate in a missionary conference.

From Europe, the brothers departed for the United States with the express purpose of recruiting teachers for South Africa. In the course of their five-week tour, they had opportunity to preach and speak at many places.

This was Charles's longest association with his renowned older brother. He soon learned to introduce himself as "not *the* Mr. Murray; I am *the other* Mr. Murray." "In the circle in which we move, Andrew is quite a lion," Charles would observe in a letter home. "He is a precious brother and very convenient to travel with. On his back, not literally but metaphorically, I get in anywhere!"

Andrew observed everything. American education, Sunday schools, general religious life, all were of interest to him. At Mt. Holyoke, they were pleased to see firsthand the way intellectual development and absolute consecration were equally pursued. Andrew seemed confirmed that God's providence had led them to this model for their own work.

Also of interest to Andrew was the ministry of Dwight L. Moody and Ira Sankey. He had read of the remarkable revivals taking place in America associated with Mr. Moody. While in Scotland, Andrew saw evidence of blessing from Moody's work throughout the country. "The spiritual atmosphere seemed brightened," he said, "and people more open to speaking of spiritual matters." "Grayheaded ministers in England and Scotland have acknowledged how much they have learned from these men," wrote Andrew. "And there are other evangelists, who have not exactly received a ministerial training, but whose enthusiasm and gifts have in many instances been highly instructive to those who are engaged in the regular ministry of the Word."

When the time arrived for Andrew and Charles to begin their voyage back to South Africa, they were not alone. Ten women had been recruited for work at the Huguenot Seminary in Wellington and plans for schools in seven more locations. Though not as many teachers were found as Andrew had hoped for, their trip proved fruitful.

And fruitful for more than the Huguenot Seminary—Andrew had written home from America concerning another growing conviction:

> All that I have heard, both in America and in Scotland, concerning the missionary enterprise has wrought in me a deeper conviction that our Church has been planted by God in South Africa with the purpose of bringing the Gospel to the heathen of the Continent of Africa; and that, if this work is to be done, we must have an institution where our sons can be trained to fulfill it.

On board with Charles, Andrew, and their ten teachers was also Reverend George Ferguson, brother of one of the original Huguenot Seminary teachers sent over from Mt. Holyoke. Like his sister, he too would invest his life for the Kingdom of God in the country of South Africa. He was coming over to head up plans for a Missionary Training

Institute to be started in Wellington. Classes began with ten students as soon as they arrived.

This institution would continue to grow in the years to come. More teachers, more students, and more buildings were added. Students there prepared for additional college studies or went directly to the mission field. By 1903, the Dutch Reformed Church would adopt the school as its own. True to Andrew's vision, the Mission Institute's graduates found their way most often to ministry among the mixed race and native populations of South Africa. Much of what the Dutch Reformed Church was able to do among these people was the result of Andrew's vision of the needs and opportunities there, if only people were found and trained to do it.

As if this were not enough, Andrew's commitment to a quality, Christ-centered education for all people would continue to show itself in new institutions. In 1898, as the fruit of the other developing institutions in Wellington, Huguenot College was opened. At the dedication service of its first building, Andrew, at this time seventy years old, gave a stirring address that summed up the importance and purpose of education.

> All knowledge and its application should be subservient to the formation of character, the training of the will, and the drawing out of all the nobler qualities of one's being. Mere acquisition of knowledge avails little if it leaves the man himself, the inward man, undeveloped. The real success of a country depends not upon its mineral or its agricultural wealth, but upon its men and its women.

13

The Time of Silence

In 1880, just three years after his return from Europe, Andrew encountered an unexpected and difficult turn to his life. The new schools were growing and drawing students from all across South Africa. He had conducted the first of his evangelistic tours around the Colony. His ministry in this Wellington pastorate seemed at the very peak of effectiveness for the Kingdom of God. Suddenly, in the midst of it all, he would see his ministry suffer and his faith tested.

Many years after this particular trial, while visiting England in 1895, Andrew was unable to receive a person who sought him for counsel. Instead, he scribbled out a note. "Here, give her this, that I have been writing down for myself," he said. "It may prove helpful."

> In time of trouble say,
> First: He brought me here; it is by His will I am in this strait place: in that I will rest.
> Next: He will keep me here in His love, and give me grace in this trial to behave as His child.

Then: He will make the trial a blessing, teaching me the lessons He intends me to learn, and working in me the grace He means to bestow.

Last: In His good time He can bring me out again—how and when He knows.

Say: *I am here*—(1) by God's appointment (2) in His keeping (3) under His training (4) for His time.

Psalm 1:15
Andrew Murray

Perhaps he had in mind a lesson he had learned forty years earlier when it looked as if his ministry were finished.

———

It seemed quite an odd thing. Sad and inexplicable. Here was the renowned minister of Wellington, Reverend Andrew Murray, unable to preach. Just fifty-one years old, Reverend Murray had served the Wellington church for only eight years at that point.

The inexplicable event was his "relaxed throat," a condition that made it impossible for Andrew to even speak, much less preach the long and fiery sermons that were his hallmark.

The problem first became noticeable toward the end of 1879. By early 1880, Andrew was away from his parish, spending time with his brother-in-law in an effort to find rest from speaking and the benefit of a different climate. These changes seemed to bring little relief. Through the course of the year, he was present at two important conferences held at Montagu and Worcester, but could only participate by having someone else read his papers. In October, when the Dutch Reformed Church Synod met in Cape Town, Andrew was unable to speak altogether. His duties as Moderator (this was the second time that he had been elected to that esteemed position) were handled by another minister. Minutes of that Synod record a motion that expressed the church body's "sincere regret that a weakness of the throat prevented him from taking an active part in its proceedings."

Things were indeed serious. In early 1881, Andrew again left his congregation for a change of climate. He spent several weeks inland in the high, dry region called "the Karoo." There he was treated by a particular doctor who hoped to effect a cure. Each day, Andrew would meet with the doctor to have his throat treated. For one ten-day period, he was to inhale a special mixture of steam and medicine twice a day.

During this time away, Andrew had continued to write. Various magazine articles and devotional tracts flowed from his pen. He produced the Dutch original of *Like Christ* as well as his first book in English, *Abide in Christ*. Without the demands of pastoral ministry, he had much time for prayerful reflection on a wide range of topics. It was also the time of the first Transvaal War for Independence. The Boer farmers were resisting British rule, and hostilities had broken out. Three children, daughters Emmie and Eliza as well as son James, were all residing near the battlefront.

By March, the doctor felt it time to halt the treatments. Andrew was to begin gradually and gently exercising his voice. And his friends and family observed some improvement in his voice. He was back to his parish in Wellington in time for Pentecost Sunday. Special services were held with a focus on missions, and a large offering was collected for the Missions Training Institute—an educational project dear to Andrew's heart. Everyone was hopeful.

In Andrew's letters while away in the Karoo, we see his first reflections on the topic of Divine Healing. He writes in a letter to Emma:

> My thoughts have been a good deal on the question of God's purpose for this long silence enforced upon me. You know what I have previously said about the two views of affliction: the one, that it is in chastisement for sin; the other, that it is in the light of the kindness and love of God. I have felt that it was a very great kindness to have such a time for the renewal of my bodily strength and of mental quiet and refreshment for the work before me.
>
> The thought has come however, whether I might not be in danger of overlooking the former aspect. I have been asking the Lord to show me what specially there is that He wants changed in my life. The general answer is a very easy one, and yet it is difficult to realize at once distinctly where and how the change is to come. What is needed is more spiritual life, more of the power of the Holy Ghost, in the life first, and then in the preaching. . . . Let us pray earnestly that our gracious God would search and try us and see whether there be any evil way in us. . . .

Murray's return to preaching and the hopefulness of his friends and congregation proved to be premature. In a December 5 letter to his brother John who was visiting family in Aberdeen, Scotland, Andrew writes, "My throat is decidedly improving. The last three Sundays I have been preaching in good tone and length, and have not suffered." Just a few weeks later, however, Andrew would again write his brother John. This time the news was less encouraging. "My throat was improving, but got put back, partly by a cold taken at Moorreesburg on the occasion of the induction of Retief, and partly owing to the strain of the New Year and prayer-week services." This "put back" turned out to be a serious relapse. All the ground gained was lost! Before winter's end, Andrew could no longer preach or even speak with his congregation. It was indeed sad and inexplicable.

The setback was so serious that by springtime, the consistory of the Wellington Church suggested that Andrew take time off to journey to Europe. There he could relax, experience a change in climate, and consult the best medical practitioners available. Arrangements were quickly made and by May of 1882, Andrew and Emma were on board a steamer for London! Though unable to speak, Andrew's heart for God's work did not flag. Just days before their departure, a silent Andrew participated in the laying of the cornerstone for the new Missionary Training Institute in Wellington.

It was obviously a time of distress and great searching. One can see that in his letters during this time of silence, Andrew's love for God, and his sense of being loved by God, seemed never to falter.

Andrew and Emma spent less than four months

in and around London. Within a week of their arrival, while pursuing medical treatment and visiting a conference at Mildmay, Andrew happened to cross paths with one of the people he was most anxious to meet. Pastor Stockmaier's writings on healing through prayer had caught Andrew's attention some years before. He and Emma had planned to travel to Switzerland to meet with this very man.

Andrew met with Stockmaier immediately.

"Pastor Stockmaier?" Andrew spoke with his weakened voice, barely audible. "I recognize that God makes a promise in James 5:15 when the Scripture says, 'And the prayer offered in faith will make the sick person well; the Lord will raise him up.' It seems to me that I am unable to reach that kind of faith. Is that because deep in my heart I might hold a secret doubt as to whether it is God's will that I should be healed? Perhaps it would bring more glory to God if I were to remain silent, and serve him in some other capacity. Are not suffering and trial a means of grace which God uses to sanctify His people?"

"Oh, Reverend Murray," replied Pastor Stockmaier with kindness. "You are still bound up by the customary view of Christians about suffering. Look again at the Scripture there. Do you see how carefully James distinguishes between 'suffering' and 'disease'? Look and see."

Andrew looked carefully at the text and continued to listen intently.

"In regard to suffering or affliction, James says 'let him pray for wisdom.' Look at it here in chapter one, verses two through five. But later on, in chapter five, verses fourteen and fifteen, we read 'Is any among you sick . . . the prayer offered in faith will make the sick person well.'

"You are right, Reverend Murray. There is no promise that we will escape the temptations and trials of this life that are the cause of much suffering. We have a different kind of promise in regard to sickness in our body."

This providential encounter was to lead Andrew further along the path of discovery. He and Pastor Stockmaier would continue to exchange ideas and study together over the next two weeks. His searching mind, his love for God, and his desperate need drove him on. He was soon delighted to discover that a newly opened residential retreat center called Bethshan, dedicated to the practice of healing prayer, had just been opened in London. He and Emma quickly checked in and began to pursue the program of daily prayer, Bible study, and small-group encouragement.

> Morning by morning the sixteen or eighteen (residents) were assembled around the Word of God, and instructed as to what there still remained in themselves to prevent them from appropriating the promise, and what there was in Scripture to encourage them to faith and to complete surrender. I cannot remember that I have ever listened to expositions of the Word of God in which greater simplicity and a more glorious spirit of faith were revealed, combined with heart-searching application of God's demand to surrender everything to Him. . . .

And in a later letter to his congregation:

> From these brief accounts you will perceive

that faith healing has a much higher aim than the mere deliverance of the body from certain maladies: it points to the road of holiness and full consecration that God would have us follow. . . .

Andrew Murray's throat was healed!

He and Emma returned to South Africa in October of 1882. Upon arrival at Wellington, he would once again be swept up into the many demands of his ministry. His brother John died unexpectedly toward the end of the year. The General Synod elected Andrew to a third term as Moderator the next year. Never again would his voice hold him back from service to the Kingdom of Christ. He was a different man in many ways. His restored throat would serve as a living reminder of the power and love of God, giving Andrew a new voice of grace in all he spoke, wrote, and did.

For another thirty years, Andrew proclaimed the Gospel of Jesus Christ in North America, Europe, and South Africa. He would preach at Keswick, minister with Moody and Sankey, and serve as Moderator of the Dutch Reformed General Synod four more times—all *after* the healing of his throat condition.

In 1884, Andrew published a book entitled *Divine Healing*. Though little known today, this volume brings the same balance, pastoral insight, and biblical basis to the subject of healing that have been the hallmarks of his writing in other areas. It is easily forgotten that most of his best-loved books, *With Christ in the School of Prayer, The State of the Church, The Two Covenants*, were written *after* his experience of healing.

Until his death, Andrew continued to teach about divine healing. For a time he even considered focusing his ministry on healing through prayer. Although Pastor Stockmaier persuaded him not to focus exclusively on this, Andrew regularly prayed for the sick and saw many, though clearly not all, healed.

Miss McGill was a longtime friend of the Murray family and had been charged with the care of their younger children during a particular trip to Europe. Andrew and Emma returned from Europe to find her seriously ill and near death. "I have lived just long enough to deliver the children to you again," she said upon their arrival.

Andrew, in the earnestness of his own newfound experience, explained to her the principles of healing and then offered prayer for her. Soon, she arose and was restored to health. For many years to follow, she served God with the YWCA in Cape Town.

In later years, Andrew had opportunity to pray for Reverend Pieter F. Hugo. Known as a truly pious and devoted Christian, Reverend Hugo was married to a niece of Andrew's and so drew his special attention. Andrew began to pray for him after Hugo developed symptoms of consumption (tuberculosis) and had to withdraw from his pastoral work. At first, there appeared to be marked improvement, and Reverend Hugo was encouraged in his faith. Andrew watched and continued to pray with him whenever they would meet at various ministers' gatherings. After a few months, Reverend Hugo weakened and suddenly died. According to one biographer it happened "on the very day when the new building of the Training Institute was opened at Wellington. His decease was a great blow to Mr. Murray, who had cherished the most confident expectation of Reverend Hugo's recovery."

From the time of his own healing on, Andrew always looked first to God for his health needs. Once, while traveling through the Natal province on an evangelistic tour, he was thrown to the ground when the ox cart he was riding in was upset. His arm was badly and visibly broken. Not to miss his preaching appointment, Andrew bandaged the arm himself, made the injury a matter of prayer, and proceeded on through the entire mission. Months later, when Andrew showed the arm to a doctor friend, the doctor assured Andrew that the break had been "most remarkably and perfectly set and healed."

For all his faith and convictions, Andrew did not disdain or, as a habit, avoid doctors, especially when requested by his family. There were occasions when Andrew was confined to his bed for some medical reason. At those times, his daughter Annie remembered, "No patient was more obedient to instructions, more cheerful in attitude, or more grateful for the least attention. . . ."

His daughter Emmie remembers well the change in her father upon his healing and return from Europe in 1882:

It was after the "time of silence," when God came so near to Father and he saw more clearly the meaning of a life of full surrender and simple faith, that he began to show in all relationships that constant tenderness and unruffled lovingkindness and unselfish thought for others which increasingly characterized his life from that point. At the same time he lost nothing of his strength and determination.

More and more was developed that wonderful, grave, and beautiful humility which could never be put on, but could only be the work of the indwelling Spirit. It was felt immediately by all who came into contact with him.

It is this transformation of character that seems to be the most important outcome from this period of Andrew's life. The humble dependence on God that Annie records should be recognized as the wellspring from which the books, preaching, and even the healing itself, would all now flow. One could easily be caught up in the joy and excitement of Andrew's restored voice and miss this. Andrew's restored voice was more than a miracle, it was a transforming experience of intimacy with God.

14

Abiding in Christ: The Later Years

The year was 1895, and the place was Keswick, England. Once again, Andrew had traveled from South Africa to England. This time he was the honored guest speaker for the annual Keswick Convention. These yearly meetings had originated in the Moody-Sankey revival of 1875, and continued through the years as a focal point for a growing movement of evangelical renewal centered on "practical holiness," prayer, and missions. Now that the children were all grown, Emma always traveled with him. She was close by his side. At the age of sixty-seven, Andrew appeared thin and frail from a distance. Up close, however, or as he preached, there was a very different perception.

"Well, of course, many of you have never heard my own testimony," declared Andrew. His voice sounded alive and strong. His words were well chosen and to the point. With a good-natured tweak for his listeners, he spoke on.

"I don't often share it!" There was a sparkle in his eye. It was not shyness or fear or belligerence that motivated his response. One could sense that even in his refusal, he had a lesson to teach.

Conversation would go on that afternoon. Those around him pressing their case, Andrew weighing his words in response.

Later that day, when Andrew entered the platform to preach at the main gathering, some were surprised to hear what he was to say. Those who had spent the afternoon with him knew that it was a word from the Master, not their requests, that moved him.

When I was asked to give my testimony I doubted whether it would be desirable, and for this reason: we all know what helpfulness there is in a clear-cut testimony of a man who can say: "There I was, I knelt down, and God helped me, and I entered in to the better Life." I cannot give such a testimony, but I know what blessing it has often brought to me to read of such testimonies for the strengthening of my own faith. And yet I got this answer from those who wished me to speak: "Perhaps there are many at Keswick to whom a testimony concerning a life of more struggle and difficulty will be helpful." If it must be so, I replied, let me tell for the glory of God how He has led me.

Some of you have heard how I have pressed upon you the two stages in the Christian life, and the step from the one to the other. The first ten years of my spiritual life were manifestly spent on the lower stage. I was a minister, I may say, as zealous and as earnest and as happy in my work as anyone, as far as love of the work was concerned. Yet, all the time, there was a burning in my heart, a dissatisfaction and restlessness inexpressible. What was the reason? I had never learned with all my theology that obedience was possible. My justification was as clear as noonday. I knew the hour in which I received from God the joy of pardon. I remember in my little room at Bloemfontein how I used to sit and think, "What is the matter? Here I am, knowing that God has justified me in the blood of Christ, but I have no power for service." My thoughts, my words, my actions, my unfaithfulness—everything troubled me. Though all around thought me one of the most earnest of men, my life was one of deep dissatisfaction. I struggled and prayed as best I could.

One day I was talking with a missionary. I do not think that he knew much of the power of sanctification himself—he would have admitted it. When we were talking and he saw my earnestness he said, "Brother, remember that when God puts a desire into your heart, He will fulfill it." That helped me; I thought of it a hundred times. I want to say the same to you who are plunging about and struggling in the quagmire of helplessness and doubt. The desire that God puts into your heart He will fulfill.

I was greatly helped about this time by reading a book called *Parable From Nature*. One of these parables presents that after the creation of the earth, on a certain day, a number of crickets met. One of them began, saying, "Oh, I feel so happy. For a time I was creeping about looking for a place to stay, but I could not find the place that suited me. At last I got in behind the bark of an old tree, and it seemed as though the place were just fitted for me, I felt so comfortable there." Another said, "I was there for a time, but it would not fit me"—that was a grass cricket. "But at last I got on to a high stalk of grass, and as I clung there and swung there, in the wind and the air, I felt that that was the place made for me." Then a third cricket said, "Well, I have tried the bark of the old tree, and I have tried the grass, but God has made no place for me, and I feel unhappy." Then the old mother cricket said, "My child, do not speak that way. Your Creator never made anyone without preparing a place for him. Wait, and you will find it in due time." Some time after, these same crickets met together again and got to talking. The old mother said, "Now, my child, what say you?" The cricket replied, "Yes, what you said is true. You know those strange people who have come here. They built a house, and in their house they had a fire; and, you know when I got into the corner of the hearth near the fire I felt so warm, that I knew that was the place God made for me."

That little parable helped me wonderfully, and I pass it on to you. If any are saying that God has not got a place for them, let them trust God, and wait, and He will help you, and show you what is your place. So the Lord led me till in His great mercy I had been eleven or twelve years in Bloemfontein. Then He brought me to another congregation in Worcester, about the time when God's Holy Spirit was being poured out in America, Scotland, and Ireland. In 1860, when I had been six months in the congregation, God poured out His Spirit there in connection with my preaching, especially as I was moving about in the country, and a very unspeakable blessing came to me. The first Dutch edition of my book *Abide in Christ* was written at that time. I would like you to understand that a minister or a Christian author may often be led to say more than he has experienced. I had not then experienced all that I wrote of; I cannot say that I experience it all perfectly even now. But if we are honest in seeking to trust God in all circumstances and always to receive the truth, He will make it live in our hearts. But let me warn you, Convention Christians, not to seek too much satisfaction in your own thoughts, or in the thoughts of others. The deepest and most beautiful thoughts cannot feed the soul; unless you go to God and let Him give you reality and faith, you cannot know satisfaction.

Well, God helped me, and for seven or eight years I went on, always enquiring and seeking, and always getting. Then came, about 1870, the great Holiness Movement. The letters that appeared in *The Revival* [magazine] touched my heart; and I was in close fellowship with what took place at Oxford and Brighton, and it all helped me. Perhaps if I were to talk of consecration I might tell you of an evening there in my own study in Cape Town. Yet I cannot say that that was my deliverance, for I was still struggling. Later on, my mind became much exercised about the baptism of the Holy Spirit, and I gave myself to God as perfectly as I could to receive the baptism of the Spirit. Yet there was failure, God forgive it. It was somehow as if I could not get what I wanted. Through all these stumblings God led me, without any very special experience that I can point to; but as I look back I do believe now that He was giving me more and more of His blessed Spirit, had I but known it better.

I can help you more, perhaps, by speaking, not of any marked experience, but by telling very simply what I think God has given me now, in contrast to the first ten years of my Christian life. In the first place, I have learned to place myself before God every day, as a vessel to be filled with His Holy Spirit. He has filled me with the blessed assurance that He, as the everlasting God, has guaranteed His own work in me. If there is one lesson that I am learning day by day, it is this: That it is God who worketh all in all. Oh, that I could help any brother or sister to realize this!

I will tell you where you fail. You have never yet heartily believed that He was working out your salvation. You believe that if a painter undertakes a picture he must look to every shade of color and every touch upon the canvas. You believe that if a workman makes a table or a bench he knows how to do his work. But you do not believe that the everlasting God is working out the image of His Son in you. As any sister here is doing a piece of ornamental or fancy work, following out the pattern in every detail, let her just think: "Can God not work out in me the purpose of His love?" If that piece of work is to be perfect, every stitch must be in its place. And remember that not one minute of your life should be without God. We want God to come in at times—say in the morning; then we are to live two or three hours, and He can come in again. No, God must be every moment the Worker in your soul.

I was once preaching, and a lady came to talk with me. She was a very pious woman, and I asked her, "How are you coming along?" Her answer was, "Oh, just the way it always is, sometimes light and sometimes dark." "My dear sister, where is that in the Bible?" I asked. She said, "We have day and night in nature, and just so it is in our souls." I said, "No, no; in the Bible we read, Your sun shall no more go down." Let me believe that I am God's child and that the Father in Christ, through the Holy Ghost, has set His love upon me, and that I may abide in His presence, not frequently, but unceasingly.

You will ask me, "Are you satisfied? Have you got all you want?" God forbid. With the deepest feeling of my soul I can say that I am satisfied with Jesus now; but there is also the consciousness of how much fuller the revelation can be of the exceeding abundance of His grace. Let us never hesitate to say, "This is only the beginning." When we are brought into the holiest of all, we are only beginning to take our right position with the Father.

May He teach us our own nothingness and transform us into the image of His Son and help us to go out to be a blessing to our fellow men. Let us trust Him and praise Him in the midst of a consciousness of failure and of a remaining tendency to sin. Notwithstanding this, let us believe that our God loves to dwell in us; and let us hope, without ceasing, in His still more abundant grace.

The Murrays traveled on from Keswick to Northfield, Massachusetts, in the United States.

There Andrew's friend Dwight L. Moody held an annual convention of his own. For two weeks, Andrew conducted the morning sessions. His focus was on the one theme that would run through his writings and messages for the rest of his life: the feeble spiritual life of God's people, and its effect on the life of the church and the work of missions. Throngs of people, including over four hundred ministers, were in attendance. From Northfield they campaigned on to Toronto, Boston, Chicago, New York, and elsewhere. Always he called God's people to a life of total surrender, complete abiding in His strength every minute of every day. With vigor, Andrew and Emma traveled on, campaigning in Holland, Ireland, and Scotland before returning home to South Africa.

At home in South Africa, Andrew's ministry continued at an amazing pace. In 1889, he had been instrumental in the founding of the Cape General Mission, an organization that sponsored Keswick-style conventions each year in South Africa. For the remaining twenty-eight years of his life, Andrew would take a special interest in these conventions. He preached there often. He prayed for God to bless them. He provided guidance and helped the church at large in South Africa to understand the value of such conventions.

All across the world at this time, there was a growing sense that each Christian could enjoy victory over sin in their own life. Conventions and publications helped spread the message of this "Deeper Life" or "Holiness Movement." Preachers like Dwight L. Moody, R. A. Torrey, Hannah Whitall Smith, and F. B. Meyer traveled extensively, sharing the message of consecration and surrender. Andrew Murray, in his own way and place, is an expression of this same tide.

Direct and to the point, Andrew preached often on the importance of each believer being filled with the Holy Spirit. One such message from the South African Keswick Convention exemplifies the clarity of his points:

> I *must* be filled. It is absolutely *necessary*.
> I *may* be filled. God has made it blessedly *possible*.
> I *would* be filled. It is eminently *desirable*.
> I *will* be filled. It is so blessedly *certain*.

Another series of fruitful endeavors in Andrew's later years were the frequent evangelistic campaigns he conducted across South Africa, some being several months long. Between 1879 and 1904, Andrew conducted nine such tours, each similar in nature to those conducted in the United States and England by Dwight L. Moody. Andrew would conduct a series of meetings in each town, often in a rented hall rather than a single church. The "after-meetings" and evangelistic thrust of the messages were not always well received by the church members of each locale. Andrew went out of his way in terms of preparation and accommodation, though, to work with local pastors and help them see the benefits of such a ministry. In the end, the abundant fruit born from this work demonstrated its value. One is amazed to think that all of this was done on nine separate occasions—through the course of two wars, his throat problems and eventual healing, his regular pastoral duties, writing, and founding schools.

Just before the Murrays left for Keswick in 1895, Andrew became increasingly drawn to the work of eighteenth-century English mystic William Law. In many respects a deep and remarkable man, Law and his book *A Serious Call to a Devout and Holy Life* had a profound effect on men like John Wesley and George Whitefield and the revivals under their ministry. Though Law held several unorthodox convictions, his emphasis on the experiential nature of religious life and the surrender of the self life attracted Andrew's attention. While admitting and rejecting Law's shortcomings, Andrew did much to bring Law's work into circulation in newly edited form, including *Freedom from the Self-Centered Life* and *The Power of the Spirit*. Had Andrew lived a century earlier in England, he would have no doubt bridged the gulf between Law's mysticism and John Wesley's activism. He embodied in his own character the best of each of those great men.

Andrew's involvement in the pastoral work of his own congregation never faltered in the midst of these many outside endeavors and interests. In fact, it was not until 1892 that an associate pastor was assigned to the Wellington congregation to work with Andrew. Reverend J. R. Albertyn was a minister of like mind and spirit with Andrew. He too would often head out into the countryside on evangelistic campaigns that bore great fruit.

One can easily imagine the trepidation that Reverend Albertyn must have felt in coming alongside such a revered man of God as Andrew Murray. Before accepting the call, he wrote asking, "What would happen if I cannot agree with you?"

"Come along, my Brother," was Andrew's reply. "I will agree with you, only be sure you are always in the right." With that beginning, the two developed a deep respect and affection for each other.

15

Your Sun Shall Not Go Down

Even a life as energetic and productive as that of Andrew Murray had to one day end.

Emma passed on in 1905, the result of a stroke. She had suffered from serious rheumatism in her later years and was confined to her bed late in 1904. On January 2, she slipped into eternity while Andrew was praying and her four daughters knelt at her bedside. As a friend of the family would write, "She passed away, sincerely mourned by all who knew and loved her, leaving to us an inspiring example of piety, patience, gentleness, Christian grace, and wholehearted devotion to Jesus Christ the Lord."

Andrew retired from active ministry the very next year at the age of 78. He resided in Wellington for the remaining ten years of his life, even preaching there until 1916. Until the very end, he continued a remarkably busy itinerary of speaking and traveling, though staying increasingly close to home.

Andrew died on January 18, 1917, at the age of

88 years and eight months.

On the last night of his life, he paused before heading off to bed. Speaking to those around in the home, he said, "We have such a great and glorious God we ought to be always rejoicing in Him."

He then prayed, saying, "Oh! Ever blessed and glorious God, satisfy us with Thy mercy that we may rejoice and be glad in Thee all our days. Satisfy me that I may rejoice and be glad always in Thee."

Later that night he began to fail. As family members took turns watching and praying at his bedside, he slipped in and out of consciousness. Once he spoke to his daughter Annie, saying, "Have faith in God, my child. Do not doubt Him." And then again, "God is worthy of trust."

Though unconscious and restless through the next day, he passed away peacefully early the next evening.

One thing that shall never die is the collection of Andrew's writings, which he continued to produce nearly until his death. Many people around the world today continue to meet him through them.

A Final Note:
Andrew Murray and Apartheid

Mention South Africa to a person in conversation, at least among Americans, and the matter of apartheid comes to mind. Talk about Andrew Murray, and soon the question will come to the fore: "What was his involvement or opinion regarding the practice of apartheid?"

There are a number of observations that could prove helpful in considering the question. At the very least, the question of Andrew Murray and apartheid is asked often enough, and with enough sincere interest, that it deserves a few comments for clarification.

First of all, some facts. Andrew Murray passed away on January 18, 1917, at the advanced age of 88 years and eight months. He had retired from an active ministry in 1906, becoming increasingly more homebound until his death.

Though racial segregation, even sanctioned by law, had been the norm in South African life, actual

apartheid laws were not institutionalized in South
Africa until 1948, when the Reunited National
Party won elections and supplanted the leadership
of war hero Jan Smuts and his United Party. The
Group Areas Act and Population Registration Act,
with its universal "pass" books and racial registration, followed in 1950, a full century after Murray's
induction as pastor in Bloemfontein. Clearly,
Andrew Murray never lived to see or respond to the
structure of apartheid as we have come to see or experience it in the last half of the twentieth century.
For all intents and purposes, Murray was a man of
the nineteenth century, a citizen of the British Em-
pire of Queen Victoria. The legal structure of apartheid, by contrast, came to fruition in the same
twentieth century that produced Hitler, Stalin, and
Pol Pot.

The next question would be something like,
"How did Andrew Murray respond to the roots of
apartheid in the South Africa of his own time?"

Any examination of Andrew Murray's life finds
him to be a man firmly placed within the cultural
setting of his own time, a very different one from
our own. There were abundant racial tensions of all
sorts in nineteenth-century South Africa. It was
the whites, Boers, and British whose antipathies
led to at least two Boer Wars. Andrew Murray's life
was probably more caught up in these racial relations than in any other.

Indian nationals came to South Africa as workers toward the second half of the century, living as
second-class citizens. Matters grew increasingly
tense as time went on and their numbers grew. Mr.

Gandhi experienced their plight firsthand at the turn of the century.

Then there were the various African tribal people—Zulu, Swazi, Xhosa, Tswana and so on. These groups found themselves at various times at war among themselves or with the settlers who had moved onto their lands. The culture of the growing urban centers was pitted against the lonely rural existence of the farmers. Then came a gold rush and the discovery of diamonds worth many fortunes. All in all, it is evident that in South Africa a very tense and diverse mix of ethnic groups, cultures, and motivations existed and still exists.

Murray lived and moved within the setting of that South Africa. He was not a social revolutionary on any matter, nor an "integrationist" on matters of race. At first glance, he seems to have simply lived and ministered within the cultural context that he was born in. A bit more depth, however, quickly produces a more refined and complex character.

First of all, Andrew Murray is an interesting figure bridging the two white cultures of South Africa—the Dutch Boers and the British. He was bilingual in his preaching and writing. A minister of the Dutch Reformed Church who won the hearts of even the most distant of the Transvaal Boers, he also represented local interests against the Abandonment of the Orange Free Sovereignty before the Crown in England in 1854.

In his mammoth biography of Murray, J. Du-Plessis devotes an entire chapter to "Andrew Murray as a South African Patriot." Through both Boer Wars, Murray's sympathies stood clearly with the Boers for independence. He recognized their yearning for national identity and rightful claim to such in the Sand River Convention of 1852. He was vocally opposed to the British duplicity in the Jameson Raid and Second Boer War concentration camps in which thousands of women and children died.

But to recognize and advocate for Boer independence and against British policy hardly means that Andrew Murray would have supported the later developments of apartheid, though these were rooted to some extent in feelings of Boer nationalist identity.

Indeed, Murray was quick to point to inept British policy as hardening Boer hearts with race hatred. Just days before the outbreak of the Second Boer War in 1899, Murray penned an impassioned appeal for peace to the British people in which he wrote:

> I cannot believe that the British people will give its sanction to a war that, even if England conquers, can end in nothing but the extinction of two free Republics, in the extermination of tens of thousands of men who are determined to die for their liberty, in the alienation of our whole people, and the perpetuation of race-hatred for generations to come.

Even more to the point, Murray, as early as 1913, identified and resisted the ideas of a man who would in fact lead the way for the system of legal apartheid.

Dr. Daniel F. Malan was a Dutch Reformed pastor who would resign his charge in order to pursue a career in politics. He represented no small sentiment in the country when he spoke, saying, "If the dissensions which divide our people are not healed, I cannot see how our Church can in the long run remain united. There is a tendency in members of the same Church to unite, not merely in confession and belief, but also in political views."

Church unity built around political belief! Murray saw in this a beginning that would lead to a bad end, though he knew not exactly where. Murray responded with a long and forceful letter.

I do not know how I can best define the divergence between these thoughts and my own conception, than by saying that I cannot in the least see that a schism in the Church is unavoidable because there exist within it two parties with different political convictions. The Church surely is a spiritual body, specially created by the Lord with the purpose of uniting in the power of a supernatural love, which derives its strength from Christ through the Holy Spirit, all His members, drawn even from nations which may have hated and despised one another. Paul gave expression more than once to the thought: "In the new man there is not Greek and Jew, circumcision and uncircumcision, Barbarian and Scythian, bondman and freeman; but Christ is all and in all" (Galatians 3:28).

Differences of opinion are not in themselves sinful. They are the result of differences of temperament, of education, of environment. In every nation there is found the distinction between Conservatives and Liberals, between men who seek safety in the retention of what is old and approved, and the men who look for salvation in what is new. Such differences of insight are indispensable for the well-being of a people. Friction helps to sharpen the mind, so that each party contributes its own share toward the ultimate issue of the conflict. *It is not the difference of viewpoint, but the sin of self-will and lovelessness that yields the bitter fruit in which dissension and hatred are revealed* (emphasis added).

Our Church has, I think, acted wisely in always seeking to emphasize that it was not her calling, nor yet that of her ministers as such, to engage in politics. One may ask then, "But ought not religion to exercise influence upon politics, and so upon everything that can be of service to society and to humanity?" Undoubtedly; but in a quite different manner. It is the calling of the Church to educate her members to take their due share as citizens of the State. She does this by teaching them to walk in the fear of God, by assisting them to shape a character that above all things is steadfast in its obedience to God's will, and in that love which lives not for itself but for its fellow men. There is a wide gulf between the conception that the Church must directly teach her members which political views are the right ones, and the thought that she must assist them to apply to practical life the great principles of the Word of God. [As regards present dissension] the Church must allow the voice of God to be heard above all the roaring of the waters: "Love one another, forbearing one another in love; as Christ hath forgiven you, even so do ye likewise." If the Church is faithful to this duty, it will be impossible that there should be any thought of disruption because of political differences.

This statement is particularly significant in that here Andrew Murray opposes the first principles of a man who would go on to become a chief architect of the legalized structure of apartheid. Malan's political career is an open case. First forming the Purified National Party, which later merged to become the Reunited National Party, Malan rose to the position of Prime Minister in the 1948 election, one where his coalition received a minority of total votes, but a majority of seats. Malan would serve in that position for another sixteen years, belligerently leading South Africa into its most turbulent years, driven by his intense Afrikaans nationalism and quest for racial purity. One is hard pressed to imagine that in the thirty years between Murray's death and Malan's rise to power, Malan's ideas or policies would have grown any more acceptable to Andrew Murray.

Of course, some would see in Murray's statement the Achilles' heel of his perspective: a separation of church life from the practice of politics. Did this lead to a kind of compartmentalized world view that made it possible for the Dutch Reformed Church to have an orthodox Christian stance with regard to doctrine while supporting apartheid in the separate realm of politics? This is the same mental gymnastic that Presbyterians in the southern Confederacy had called the "spirituality of the church" in their rationalization of slavery before the American Civil War.

This may well have been the fatal flaw for the generations following Murray. It seems hardly to have been the case for his own life, however. As we observe during his Cape Town pastorate, Murray would resist the entanglement of the secular government in the life and ministry of the church when it came to matters of faith and discipline. To Andrew Murray, separate spheres for church and government did not mean a church subservient to any government. Indeed, a clear distinction between the two spheres could be used to give the church a position from which to speak positively and prophetically to a government that had turned from God's purposes. Such an opportunity would appear just a few decades later. In 1934, Karl Barth and the German Confessing Church would write the Barmen Declaration to expose and denounce the Nazi commandeering of the German State Church based on just such a distinction.

Murray's vision here is not of an isolated church, safe and removed from the dirty world of politics and compromise, whose people share a common doctrine or experience inside the church building, then go their separate ways outside. Instead, he called people to a church life so transformed by the power of Christ's love that the reconciliation which first occurred in the church would spill out into all other spheres of life. For Murray, it was the church that affected the people who affected the government, not the church that affected the government. For him, personal transformation was the key to corporate transformation. No state could be righteous apart from righteous citizens. Any state whose citizens have found reconciliation through Christ in their church will live out reconciled life in the body politic.

Nor would the church ever be merely a reinforcement of one's cultural heritage. Andrew Murray regularly turned away from church membership candidates who lacked an authentic experience of Christ. Being Boer was never enough for Reverend Murray. One must be born again!

Another question to pursue could be phrased, "How did Andrew Murray act in his own contact with different races?"

Again, we must say that he was a man of his times. For the most part he accepted the structures of interaction between various peoples as they were.

Both his family and his in-laws were progressive and active in opposition of slavery.

Murray never debased himself by dehumanizing other races, which is the first step toward the rationalizing of all manner of brutality. He recognized all people as objects of God's redeeming love in Christ. We get an interesting glimpse of this, and insight into the atmosphere of his family, in an 1862 letter to his children:

> Perhaps Mama has told you that some of the white people here do not wish the black people to be taught about Jesus. This is because they do not love Him themselves. But Mr. Kruger [Paul Kruger, child of the *Great Trek* and ardent advocate of Boer independence from Britain; Kruger would become president of the Transvaal during the turbulent Gold Rush and Boer War] says that when God gave him a new heart, it was as if he wanted to tell everyone about Jesus' love, and as if he wanted the birds and the trees and everything to help him praise his Savior; and so he could not bear that there should be any poor black people not

knowing and loving the Savior whom he loved.

One can understand how two of his own sons would come to give their lives as missionaries, spreading the Gospel among African tribal people.

Murray does speak directly, though rarely, to the issue of racism in his writings. In a devotional article entitled "Race Hatred" (September 13, of the yearly devotional *God's Best Secrets*; or Reading #8 in the Pocket Companion Series entitled *The Secret of Brotherly Love*), Murray has this interesting statement:

> No wonder that man's love of his own people, implanted in his heart by nature, soon changed to hatred of other peoples. Love of country became the fruitful source of race-hatred, war, and bloodshed. Note how, here in South Africa, God has placed the two races (Andrew may well have meant Boer and British) side by side, as in a school, to see if our Christianity will enable us to overcome race-hatred and in the power of Christ's love prove that "in the new creature there is neither Greek nor Jew, barbarian nor Scythian, bond nor free, but are all one in Christ Jesus" [Galatians 3:28].
>
> What an opening there is for the Church of Christ and her ministers to preach and proclaim the love of God and to prove its might to change race-hatred into brotherly love! God has abundant power to bring this to pass.

One can hardly find in Andrew Murray even the seeds of the racial views and practices that would come to fruition in the legal structure of apartheid. He was more concerned with the *souls* of people, and the evil that comes from them, than the structures of a society and the evil that those structures instill in people's hearts. We must also keep in mind that the South African frontier where he began his ministry in 1849 was dramatically different in terms of economy, demography, and history than the South Africa that birthed apartheid a century later.

Regardless of how we finally answer the question of Andrew Murray and apartheid, we ought at least to be reminded that faithfulness to God is a daily challenge for each generation. No matter how faithful or fallen our forbearers, the challenge facing each of us is the call to faithfulness *today*, right where we are. The legacy of Andrew Murray ought to be judged in how he helps us do that.

Author's Note

I remember the very place and time, fifteen years ago, when I read the first chapter of *The Believer's Prayer Life* entitled "The Sin of Prayerlessness." It changed my life. I was earnestly convicted, but not condemned. I saw the problem with my prayer life in the same instant that I saw the solution. I was called higher and shown the stairsteps.

Since that time, I have continued to collect and read, or better pray, through as many of Andrew Murray's writings as possible. The seed for this book was planted one day when I realized how much I had come to know of Jesus through Andrew Murray, and how little I had come to know of Mr. Murray.

Of course, Andrew would want it that way, and I respect that. But I have found that as I have learned more about the situations and circumstances surrounding Andrew's walk with God, I have been better able to appreciate Andrew's lessons from God.

I hope this book does the same for you.

A special word of thanks to all who helped this book become a reality: my parents, Bill and Audrey, and family, Mary Lynn, Nicole, Rachel and William; those who across many years have taught me and let me learn (more than I can name!); my staff and the people of Mt. Pleasant Community Church and First Presbyterian Church in Houma, Louisiana; and Gordon-Conwell Theological Seminary, where this book first took shape as a D.Min. dissertation.